Photography Business

How to Start Your Own Company and Thrive

(A Beginner's Guide to Starting a Successful Business as a Photographer)

Troy Buchanan

Published By **Darby Connor**

Troy Buchanan

Photography Business: How to Start Your Own Company and Thrive (A Beginner's Guide to Starting a Successful Business as a Photographer)

ISBN 978-1-9992856-7-8

No part of this guidebook shall be reproduced in any form without permission in writing from the publisher except in the case of brief quotations embodied in critical articles or reviews.

Legal & Disclaimer

The information contained in this book is not designed to replace or take the place of any form of medicine or professional medical advice. The information in this book has been provided for educational & entertainment purposes only.

The information contained in this book has been compiled from sources deemed reliable, and it is accurate to the best of the Author's knowledge; however, the Author cannot guarantee its accuracy and validity and cannot be held liable for any errors or omissions. Changes are periodically made to this book. You must consult your doctor or get professional medical advice before using any of the suggested remedies, techniques, or information in this book.

Upon using the information contained in this book, you agree to hold harmless the Author from and against any damages, costs, and expenses, including any legal fees potentially resulting from the application of any of the information provided by this guide. This disclaimer applies to any damages or injury caused by the use and application, whether directly or indirectly, of any advice or information presented, whether for breach of contract, tort, negligence, personal injury, criminal intent, or under any other cause of action.

You agree to accept all risks of using the information presented inside this book. You need to consult a professional medical practitioner in order to ensure you are both able and healthy enough to participate in this program.

Table Of Contents

Chapter 1: Failing To Take Care Of Legal

Failing to take care of prison and felony responsibility troubles on the same time as you start a snap shots corporation can be a highly-priced mistake. When starting your images corporation, you'll need to hold in mind many jail troubles. Here's a examine a number of the vital crook and legal responsibility problems that need to be addressed at the identical time as you get started out.

Business Name – When beginning your pictures corporation, you'll want to decide on a employer name. It's important to make sure that the decision you want to apply isn't already in use with the aid of means of each extraordinary employer. You can run a call looking for with the right nation company, and if you discover that your business enterprise call isn't in use, it's viable to reserve that call at the same time as you're beginning your commercial agency and focusing on different employer issues.

Choosing a Business Structure – It's moreover essential to choose out the kind and form of business enterprise you want to apply to your photos commercial business enterprise. You have more than one company structures to select from, alongside a restricted jail obligation employer, S-organization, partnership, sole-proprietorship, employer, or restricted partnership. To figure out which preference is quality, recollect the legal duty troubles that may be related to starting your snap shots agency, as well as which possibility offers the pleasant tax structure on your industrial agency desires.

Business Licenses – At a minimal, you'll at least need tax registration and a commercial organisation license to start your personal snap shots commercial enterprise.

Local municipalities may additionally moreover have particular licensing necessities that you may want to meet as nicely. Before you begin your enterprise, make sure you have the company licenses needed to avoid prison issues.

Liability Insurance – You'll furthermore need to spend money on a preferred prison responsibility coverage coverage. If a consumer suffers bodily accidents on the identical time as at your studio, that customer want to gather for pain and suffering, misplaced wages, clinical payments, and extra. Your photographs enterprise may be liable for damages apart from physical injuries as well, which consist of slander and libel. A famous felony responsibility insurance gives your pics enterprise business employer with coverage for judgments that relate to damage complaints up for your coverage's limits, and people policies moreover cover the rate of legal protection. Many potential injuries to clients are covered with the useful resource of those pointers, together with harm from a physical item on the business enterprise premises or slipping and falling on your studio.

Even when you have your enterprise hooked up as a limited legal responsibility enterprise, elegant legal duty coverage remains an remarkable idea. While a restrained felony responsibility organization continues you in my view included, a criminal hassle notwithstanding the reality that have to bring about damages that would turn out to be bankrupting your enterprise in case you didn't have legal responsibility coverage.

Contracts – If you plan to use contracts on your photography business enterprise, it's an extraordinary idea to have an first rate criminal expert assist you write up a extraordinary settlement. Not best ought to an jail expert write your contracts, but you need to additionally use an attorney that is familiar with the pictures business organization.

While it is able to be high priced to have the settlement written up by way of an prison professional, you'll be capable of use that settlement over and over to your business enterprise.

Unfortunately, many photographers never reflect onconsideration on the jail and liability issues concerned in starting a commercial enterprise enterprise corporation until they've got a hassle.

Make sure you deal with those problems early to make sure that you and your organization are protected.

Photography Business Mistake – Not Understanding the Costs Involved in Running a Photography Business Previously, we noted how costly it may be to use virtual photographs, specifically for the purpose that maximum people have the idea that virtual snap shots is inexpensive than film photographs. Not best is it vital to recognize all the fees concerned in the utilization of virtual pictures, however you want to understand the charges which might be involved in running a images business enterprise itself. Most new photographers don't realise how plenty it is able to price to get a pictures commercial agency walking, not to mention, the rate of retaining that business company going for walks smoothly.

It's impossible to run your pictures business business enterprise clearly. You can't really start a net net web page and start handling your enterprise agency at the internet website.

You'll need an workplace wherein you may get paintings done. Don't count on that you may truly carry out your commercial enterprise from your residing room.

Of course, you moreover mght need a studio wherein you may shoot photos of your customers. If you want to rent location in your workplace and studio, you'll be paying monthly condo fees. You'll additionally want to pay for strength and one-of-a-kind utilities in your administrative center and studio. Those might be unique monthly expenses.

We already stated some of the prices that include shopping for device. After all, you'll want a digital digital camera, a superb laptop, a tripod stand, reflectors, flash lighting fixtures, lenses, curtains, and extra.

If you're taking some photographs on internet internet page, which includes wedding ceremony pictures, in any other case you do viewing intervals on the homes of your customers, then you definately need to don't forget excursion fees. Not only will you have gas costs, however you'll moreover be placing put on and tear to your automobile, which will require protection. You'll possibly should eat at the identical time as you're on the street masses, which will become a organization fee.

Here's a observe some of the other prices that photographers fail to don't forget while beginning their pictures organisation:

Accounting Services – Dealing with taxes can be difficult in case you're new to jogging a industrial enterprise, so that you may additionally moreover want to pay for accounting offerings to help with occasional questions and yr-give up tax filing.

Business Insurance – You'll want to insure your enterprise business corporation, which incorporates restrained crook duty coverage. You may additionally moreover need insurance for your business enterprise property.

Client and Money Manager – It's crucial to have software program that helps you to song customers and employer rate variety.

Cost of Incorporation – Don't forget, to get commenced out, you'll need to pay to encompass your corporation.

Credit Card Fees – If you accept credit rating playing playing cards, you could come to be paying expenses to accept credit score gambling cards.

Licenses – The licenses you'll want in your commercial enterprise enterprise aren't free, so you'll want to make an funding. Some licenses will need to be renewed periodically, so this could turn out to be a ordinary fee.

Maintenance and Repairs – Don't forget that subjects break, and if a few aspect vital breaks, you'll need to have it repaired. Make positive you've got room in your budget for emergency protection and maintenance.

Why is it so critical to recognize the price of doing commercial business enterprise? If you don't recognize how a good buy it expenses in case you want to do enterprise, you won't be capable of price your services so you make enough cash. Fully facts how an entire lot you'll spend to begin and maintain your corporation will permit you to plot your expenses so that you cowl your prices and now have cash to pay yourself the earnings you want.

Phone Service — Whether you decide to use a landline or a cell phone to your industrial commercial enterprise company, you'll must pay your smartphone bill month-to-month.

Product Samples — Clients are less probable to purchase your products if they will be capable of't see them, so you'll need to invest in samples of the products which you plan to sell.

Website Costs — A net internet site is an essential tool to your photos corporation, and you'll want to pay every three hundred and sixty five days costs for your area call and net web website hosting. If you don't understand a manner to assemble a great website, you could need to pay someone else to construct the internet website for you.

NOT HAVING AN INCOME GOAL

Another not unusual mistake photographers make isn't always having an profits intention. If you don't recognize how lots cash you need to make, it's easy to go together with the go with the flow alongside with out ever enhancing your state of affairs financially. If you need to increase your income, you want to start thinking about how masses you realistically want to earn.

While it'd sound brilliant to make one million dollars within the first twelve months of your commercial enterprise, you still want to be sensible at the equal time as putting an profits motive. You don't need to select out a determine that is so high that you recognize you'll by no means acquire it. However, you don't want to pick out an earnings cause that undervalues your images.

Having an earnings aim is critical for severa reasons. First, setting wants to your company is vital. They encourage you and help you obtain for the matters that you really want. Having an income purpose may also can help you discern out how an entire lot artwork you need to do and the prices that you want to charge to acquire your financial desires.

Once you have your very very very own profits intention, you could determine out what number of image intervals you'll need to do to fulfill that purpose. You'll be able to decide out how lots you'll need to make from every session to fulfill that cause.

Essentially, information what you need to make will help you endorse special areas of your agency that will help you make the cash that you need.

If you in no way make an income cause, you'll never make your organization prevail. You also won't recognize how difficult you want to art work to reap achievement. You won't realize a manner to fee your services and products to make an low fee earnings. Make fine making a decision on an profits intention early and use it to gain the fulfillment you need collectively along side your pix business company.

FAILURE TO FOCUS ON IN PERSON SALES

Many photographers who begin their non-public industrial agency use the "shoot and burn" approach we mentioned earlier on this bankruptcy. They truely shoot a consultation for an exceptionally low fee and hand customers a disc with all of the virtual negatives.

Along with the "shoot and burn" mistake, those photographers are also making the error of failing to awareness on in character income.

Don't anticipate that you are assembly the dreams of your customers through the usage of handing them a disc of photographs. Not best are you failing to meet your clients' desires, you're failing to satisfy your economic wishes as a photographer. Your fine customers, those who simply price pics, want to maintain the ones recollections. They don't surely want a disc of photographs; they want someone who will help them discover merchandise with a view to hold those high-quality memories in specific strategies that healthy their way of life.

If you hand customers a disc of your images, they possibly obtained't make a purchase. It received't be due to the fact they don't much like the photos. They may not recognize what merchandise to shop for. They might also moreover additionally want to make a purchase, but life receives busy and they overlook. Your clients in fact want to shop for from you, but it's up to you to make that appear. You want to hobby on in man or woman profits.

Why do many photographers fail to consciousness on in individual income? Some new photographers don't understand that during man or woman income is the gold mine of pictures. Other photographers are too scared to even try in character income. It's time to prevent making excuses. Here are some of the not unusual excuses photographers use to keep away from in character earnings:

I don't have the time to take a seat down and do viewing training with my clients.

I don't want to harass or offend my clients.

I don't want to make my customers experience like they're being pressured.

I'm afraid they received't like the photos and I'll need to deal with my customers' disappointment.

I'm an artist and I don't need to learn how to marketplace and promote to my clients.

My pictures is good sufficient to sell itself.

No rely what your excuse is, you're incorrect. In man or woman income is the crucial component to the fulfillment of your images enterprise organisation.

Let's look at a number of the ones excuses and debunk them. The idea that during character earnings pressures, annoys, or offends customers is stupid. In individual income surely gives you a way to transport above and beyond to your customers. In reality, many clients will appreciate you taking the time to walk them through the photographs, helping them make picks together together along with your professional opinion.

Another invalid excuse is that you don't have the time for in character sales. The time you spend doing in individual income has the potential to seriously boom the amount of cash which you are making. You gained't want to shoot as many classes when you have interaction in in character earnings.

Sure, pictures is an paintings. You may be an artist, but in case you plan to make cash with your artwork, you do want to discover ways to marketplace and sell on your clients. Marketing and promoting are two of the most important necessities you want to make a pics business employer a success. If you don't apprehend the manner to promote and market and also you refuse to have a observe, your business enterprise will skip down in flames, irrespective of how extraordinary your pictures is.

A FEW MORE PHOTOGRAPHY BUSINESS MISTAKES YOU NEED TO AVOID

We've already included most of the huge pics corporation mistakes that new photographers make. However, right right here's a have a have a observe some extra mistakes you ought to keep away from in case you want to run a successful pictures organisation.

Failure to Think Long Term

Don't make the mistake of failing to suppose long term. This is a commonplace mistake amongst folks that commonly will be inclined to take every day as it comes, but you have to think about the destiny whilst you're walking a organisation.

Once you start your pics commercial agency and also you begin bringing in clients, don't start fun. The photographs enterprise is mutable, aggressive, and requires that you constantly enhance your talents, every in photographs and business corporation control.

Engage in sports activities nowadays so that it will benefit your company in the long term. For example, you could deliver clients small gadgets to thank them for his or her employer, that may flip that purchaser right into a repeat customer. Take time to beautify your abilties, as a manner to will can help you charge more for your competencies in the future. Try taking pics in new genres so that you can branch out together with your business company. Don't truely attention on nowadays; attention at the achievement of your corporation nowadays and in the destiny.

Chapter 2: Mixing Up Selling And Marketing

It's easy to mix up selling and advertising, but if you make this error, it'll rate you. Here's an example of mixing up selling and advertising. A photographer lets in the customers to position up their pics on-line with a reason to reveal them to all their buddies, questioning that this could provide them more organisation because it's loose advertising. Unfortunately, this is an example of "pass thinking," perplexing the earnings components of a images commercial company with the advertising components of the agency.

After you shoot a photo consultation, you ought to be that specialize in doing an amazing income presentation that connects collectively along with your clients on an emotional stage. This is all approximately developing a sale. When you shoot a session for your customers, you shouldn't be focused on advertising and marketing and advertising; you need to be focusing on making income. Simply sending customers home with a disc of proofs or posting their snap shots for easy get admission to on line isn't going to get you the income that they want.

Differentiate among selling and advertising and advertising and marketing while on foot your pics enterprise employer. Use the photographs you're taking for a customer that will help you make a sale. You can use certainly one of a type marketing strategies. Don't get advertising and marketing and promoting careworn otherwise you'll make awful industrial enterprise picks.

Taking Advice from the Wrong People

When you start a images business corporation, all people has recommendation for you. You'll start getting unsolicited recommendation from friends and circle of relatives contributors.

The mistake is to take all the recommendation that you are given. Don't permit really every person to persuade you and your commercial business enterprise.

Who should you are taking recommendation from? Take advice from folks which can be already wherein you need to be. If they're already a achievement and in which you want to be, then they may offer you advice that you can definitely use.

However, if you take recommendation from people who aren't in which you need to be, that recommendation truely acquired't assist you get to in which you need to be. Be cautious who you're taking advice from, and don't allow simply everybody affect your selections as you decide to expose your pictures enterprise proper into a a success one.

Thinking That Success Will Be Easy

The cause that such plenty of photographers fail is due to the truth they begin a pictures commercial enterprise with the idea that it will all be clean. They aren't organized to do the hard paintings required to assemble a a achievement commercial enterprise.

The truth is that it's in no way clean to run a business, irrespective of what type of corporation you need to run. There aren't any "get rich quick" schemes for pix businesses. There's no longer an easy manner to advantage achievement. While there are numerous topics you may do to increase profits and accumulate success, it all takes hard paintings.

Many photographers assume that achievement can be clean because of the fact they love the photos side of their business. They love clicking the shutter and taking adorable snap shots. However, the real images is handiest a small a part of taking walks your photographs business enterprise. You may be an amazing photographer, but if you're now not willing to artwork and you're not inclined to analyze the fundamentals of jogging a employer, your employer is assured to fail.

Only 20% of your commercial company efforts will consist of clicking the shutter. The special 80% of your business agency efforts will consist of accounting, advertising, promoting, and making plans. These matters may not be as amusing as the real photographs, however they are crucial to the achievement of your enterprise.

To ensure your be successful, don't begin your snap shots corporation thinking that it's far going to be easy. Don't buy in to "get rich quick" schemes. Be equipped to artwork hard. Be prepared to investigate. Be prepared to run a business enterprise. Success is possible, but you have to need it, you want to work for it. It's now not smooth, however in case you're willing to paintings tough each day, you may accomplish your goals and dreams in the pix business organisation.

Yes, it's crucial to comprehend what to do at the same time as you start a photography commercial corporation, however it's further important to comprehend what NOT to do even as you get your agency started out out. Learn from the errors of others so that you don't make high-priced mistakes your self.

When you start your pictures industrial company, you don't want to fail internal a 365 days or . You don't need to turn out to be handling burnout due to the reality you determine so difficult without growing a profits.

Build Your Business Foundation First

The records from this number one bankruptcy is lots to download and can appear daunting in advance than the whole thing. You may be feeling a touch crushed with all of the first steps you want to take to construct a a fulfillment and profitable photos enterprise. Don't fear, you're precisely in that you want to be, with starting to put together your enterprise basis. Make it your organization to keep away from those commonplace mistakes. Simply preserving off the most common mistakes will increase the opportunities that your business organisation will be successful.

Remember, we ought to first assemble a strong basis via tearing down the ones vintage partitions of commonplace mistakes, to assemble a organization that is successful and profitable. Now is the time to get your basis set in place.

SETTING GOALS, CREATING A PLAN OF ACTION, AND MAKING A DAILY SCHEDULE

Now that we have got knocked down some of the ones vintage partitions housing commonplace errors that preserve us again from being certainly a fulfillment, allow's start to bring together our "new residence" of a a success and worthwhile images business agency, starting with our desires and strategies. One of the principle advantages of beginning your non-public pictures organisation is the threat to be on pinnacle of factors of your very very very own income, time, and destiny.

Being your very very own boss sounds notable and being on top of things of some time and how you spend it sounds amazing! You probably love the concept of preserving your destiny in your arms, but maximum photographers do not recognize that the reality of strolling a agency is a lot terrific from the perception of walking your very very own company. In truth, maximum small organizations will fail within the first years, and this rapid failure is even more common inside the photographs enterprise.

If you need to make your pix enterprise a achievement, you need to change the manner you reflect onconsideration on walking your images commercial employer.

Successful marketers and industrial company owners observe very unique systems, steps, and paths which may be pretty distinct from what you might consider. If you start your pix commercial enterprise dreaming about the benefits of getting no shape and all of the time that you could take off, you're simply going to fail. There is not any magic trick you may use to make your snap shots agency succeed. You will no longer discover a get-rich-brief scheme that in reality works. Real success exceptional takes region even as you figure difficult using confirmed strategies and techniques that other a hit people have already used to advantage achievement.

Do no longer allow your ego get in the manner of your success. Do not expect that you may take over the sector, particularly in case you do not understand the basics of on foot a enterprise commercial enterprise business enterprise. You are the boss, due to this you need to preserve your self responsible. If you do no longer enjoy like rolling out of bed in recent times, you don't need to, but that preference is going to have an impact on you and your industrial corporation.

That preference may be a step that places you in the course of failure. Each day, you could make selections. The alternatives you are making will both take you inside the direction of organisation fulfillment or in the course of agency failure. The extra time you spend being unproductive and unfocused, the more difficult it will in all likelihood be to make your pics industrial business enterprise achieve success.

Remember, each second you spend jogging for your photographs business enterprise need to be handled like a billable hour. If you've got got a cause to make $two hundred,000 this year and you advise to paintings 2,000 hours this year, than each hour you're going for walks has a particular fee. With those numbers, an hour of time is properly nicely worth $100.

Every mission you whole at some stage in your operating hours must be at the $a hundred in line with hour degree. Take a minute and keep in mind that. Spending a while commenting to your pals' posts on Facebook or sorting out cool movie star pics on Instagram probable will not be taken into consideration the awesome use of some time if you're focusing on obligations that keep you at the $one hundred in step with hour degree.

This is a lot to do not forget...However here is the coolest statistics: You can be a success in case you're willing to paintings difficult and examine validated strategies of fulfillment. This begins offevolved with the manner we set our dreams. Before we get into the nitty gritty of cause putting, I want to share this quote with you. Think about the way it applies to the strength of will and perseverance you should need to run a a success and profitable photos business enterprise.

"Every morning in Africa, a gazelle wakes up. It is privy to it have to outrun the fastest lion or it will likely be killed. Every morning in Africa, a lion wakes up. It is privy to it need to run faster than the slowest gazelle, or it's going to starve. It couldn't depend whether or not you are the lion or the gazelle-at the same time as the sun comes up, you will better be walking."

SETTING GOALS FOR YOUR PHOTOGRAPHY BUSINESS

First topics first together along with your pics commercial enterprise: You want to determine out your motive. What do you need to perform? What are your quick and long time goals? Setting wants to your images business enterprise will help you create a a success advertising and marketing strategy. The short term desires you place must assist lead you on a direction within the route of undertaking your long term goals. Every company choice you are making every day ought to be primarily based totally on whether or not or no longer they help take you closer within the route of your goals.

Why Should You Set Goals?

You've in all likelihood heard lots about putting dreams within the path of your life, however maybe you're no longer effective why setting desires is so critical. Goal placing is important for the fulfillment of your photos industrial organisation for some of reasons. Some of the motives you need to set goals for your company consist of:

Goals Keep You Motivated – Setting dreams allows push you in advance and goals will preserve you affected as nicely.

When you write down your desires, you have got a written example of your internal goals, which constantly remind you of all you want to perform. When you begin running in the path of your photographs industrial organization goals, it's clean to get excited and start operating tough, however in the end, your motivation can wane.

Having goals you could visualize and attention on will maintain you related for your organisation desires, supporting you live added about to work thru instances at the identical time as your awareness starts offevolved to diminish.

Goals Fuel Your Ambition – You can even find out that dreams can gas your ambition. Goals aren't pretty tons growing a plan for your corporation – they assist come up with the inspiration to carry out great topics collectively in conjunction with your enterprise agency. If you want to accomplish subjects together with your industrial business enterprise that maximum photographers best dream about, you want to set goals and then artwork every day in the route of attaining them. As you positioned desires and observe your self making progress toward them, you will gas your ambition and also you'll ensure that your aspirations are more than virtually indistinct notions floating internal your head.

Goals Help Keep You Accountable – Goals help hold you responsible. Having dreams offers you a concrete have a test whether or not you're carrying out what you need or in case you're slacking off. If you have dreams and also you look lower again and recognize you have not made sufficient development, you may be able to realize that what you're presently doing isn't running, because of this you need to make a few adjustments. If you do now not make your self responsible, you'll have a hard time reaching achievement together with your pics commercial enterprise.

Goals Let You Know What You Really Want – Setting desires will help you determine out what you really need from your business organisation. Wandering through life with indistinct notions of feat and fulfillment will now not assist you determine out what virtually brings you happiness and success. Regularly asking your self what you want and generally reassessing your desires will make it less difficult to determine out what you really want, with a purpose to inspire you to get available, and paintings tough closer to accomplishing the ones dreams.

Goals Help You Meet Financial Targets – Of route, earnings is an intrinsic part of your photos business employer, and having correct desires will permit you to to ensure you meet your monetary goals.

Setting right business enterprise goals will assist you decide out the strive which you want to make to satisfy your profits desires.

Goals Attract New Clients — Setting particular dreams in your photographs business enterprise moreover draws new customers. When you have were given desires on your agency, they'll permit customers understand that they'll benefit from running collectively along with your commercial business enterprise. Goal setting may be very critical in cementing relationships together together with your customers.

Chapter 3: Setting Realistic Obtainable Goals

Not best do you need to set specific desires, but you furthermore may want to make sure which you set dreams which can be practical and to be had. If the dreams are not realistic and to be had, you'll by no means acquire them.

Realistic Goals – A realistic cause is a goal within the direction of that you are succesful and inclined to art work. Remember, desires may be practical and immoderate, however you're the excellent person who can figure out how excessive to set your purpose. In some times, a higher aim may be a great deal much less hard to gain than a low intention, because of the truth low desires handiest exert low motivational stress.

Attainable Goals – Once you grow to be aware of desires which is probably critical to you and your pics industrial employer, you may begin searching out strategies to reap those goals. You will start developing the economic ability, skills, attitudes, and skills you want to achieve those them. You may even begin seeing possibilities you formerly ignored to help you get within the direction of attractive in the ones dreams. If you advocate the stairs as it should be and give you a time body to carry out those steps, it's viable to reap nearly any goal which you set for yourself. Goals that might have appeared out of attain and an extended manner away start moving nearer and becoming greater conceivable, now not because the goals are becoming smaller, however due to the reality you have were given improved and grown to match them.

MAKE SURE YOU SET BUSINESS AND PERSONAL GOALS

It's critical to set every business agency goals in addition to personal goals. Many pushed agency humans make the error of excellent specializing in enterprise corporation desires, letting exceptional regions in their existence bypass. Unfortunately, this frequently effects in feeling unfulfilled later in lifestyles. You need to preserve your life properly rounded, so set enterprise and private goals that solution questions, which include: What do I want to achieve with my images corporation? What do I need out of my life? What do I need for me and my family?

Business Goals — Your business agency dreams describe what you want from your snap shots business. However, preserve in thoughts that your business employer goals are not an result in themselves. The complete reason of placing industrial business business enterprise goals is to help you accumulate your personal desires. For example, maybe you would love to growth your amazing of living or make sufficient cash to excursion extra. This may lead you to set wants to generate more money collectively together with your photographs business company. Some famous business enterprise desires that you could want to set encompass:

Financial or income desires

Improving purchaser satisfaction

Increasing your amount of sales

Skill building or learning dreams

Personal Goals – Establishing private dreams gives you a basis on your business enterprise goals. For proper achievement you need a stability among your art work and personal existence, so ensure you region accurate personal goals that reflect this. These goals have to moderate you up! Some examples of personal desires embody:

Being part of a loving circle of relatives

Having a circle of depended on buddies

Having a wholesome intellectual and emotional thoughts-set

Having an concerned, lively spiritual/non secular existence

Living a colorful and healthy lifestyles

CREATING A PLAN OF ACTION TO HELP YOU MEET YOUR GOALS

Once you have got set your desires, it's time to begin developing a direction of action to help you to fulfill them. Many small enterprise organization owners should obtain a factor in which they understand they can't run their organisation emotionally. Business want to be business employer. Trying to run a pictures agency together with your coronary coronary heart is first-class going to result in a coronary coronary heart attack.

Creating an great route of movement calls for severa steps. If you need your business corporation to attain achievement, you can need to draw customers that recognize and price your photos services and products. Here is a observe the stairs you need to take to create a super course of motion to help you obtain the dreams you've got were given to your photography organisation.

Assess Your Life Today

The first actual step you need to take in case you want to create a course of action is to evaluate your existence these days. You want to comprehend in that you stand in recent times and take ownership of your present day life. It's now not smooth, however you need to permit pass of your ego and spend a while being honest with yourself.

One of the first-rate methods to evaluate your lifestyles in recent times is to spend some time writing down your strengths and weaknesses. Do not sincerely listing them to your thoughts surely write them down so you have a seen representation and a few issue you could appearance once more at as you parent to enhance your self. There Is Great Power in Written Words VS Keeping Thoughts in Your Mind

Make effective which you write down your strengths and weaknesses in all areas of going for walks a commercial enterprise. What are your strengths and weaknesses in coping with price range? What are your strengths and weaknesses close to the every day obligations of strolling a agency? What are your strengths and weaknesses with reference to your images talents? What are your strengths and weaknesses in my opinion which could affect your capability to run your images enterprise enterprise?

If you want to map out your journey in the course of your dreams, you need to recognize wherein you're starting. You ought to understand wherein you are these days.

Make exceptional which you do now not flip to others at the identical time as you're assessing your lifestyles nowadays. Not all of us is on the equal place on the adventure. It's clean to be stimulated via specific people that you don't forget, but at the same time as you're assessing your life, it's your sincere opinion that is the maximum crucial.

Make a 1 Year Anniversary Goal

Once you have assessed your lifestyles and figure out in which you're these days, now it's time to make dreams for the following

3 hundred and sixty 5 days. Instead of jogging on a aim for December thirty first, make a 12 months anniversary reason from in recent times's date. It's crucial to have precise goals and a specific timeline for completing the dreams, but your dreams also can require some evaluation and adjustment alongside the manner.

Why make a three hundred and sixty five days anniversary reason? If you are making dreams that start January 1st and quit December thirty first, it's greater like making New Year's resolutions. Just reflect onconsideration on it − how many New Year's resolutions are in reality finished? Not many. The three hundred and sixty five days anniversary motive is a higher choice to help you create a selected date via which you want to acquire your desires.

Reviewing Goals Daily

When you placed dreams, it's essential to ensure that you evaluation them daily. Daily evaluation is crucial for several reasons. First, each day evaluation will assist you keep the ones dreams to your mind all the time. You want to be reminded of your goals each day so you understand what you're walking within the course of. Another purpose that you want to test your goals every day is to look the manner you're doing on sporting out those dreams. Sometimes you could find out which you're certainly progressing ahead of time desk. In extremely good times, you could have dealt with an unexpected setback. Both of these conditions are very commonplace whilst you're strolling inside the route of your pics business enterprise dreams.

Do not surrender in your goals! When you be aware that you had a setback, don't permit it shake your self warranty.

Celebrate the instances you've got made greater development within the path of your goals. Simply make the effort to assess in which you are, make any changes which may be desired, after which get your recognition ahead on attaining those desires.

Break Down Goals right into a Scalable Reality

Now it's time to break down your dreams proper into a scalable reality. You already comprehend what your desires are, so that you need to begin breaking them down into smaller chunks or milestones to help you accomplish your big desires. Simply announcing that you need to make $ hundred,000 in a three hundred and sixty five days looks as if a large intention. However, at the same time as you harm it down into how hundreds you need to make month-to-month and what form of you need to make weekly to benefit that aim, it turns into a good buy greater realistic. Then, you can determine out what obligations you need to do every day to gain the ones smaller milestones that assist you eventually benefit your big goals.

Figuring Out the Net Amount of Money You Need to Make

Let's take a look at the financial dreams which you have set for the subsequent 12 months. What does your internet income need to be that permits you to acquire the ones financial goals? How masses do you need to make every month to accumulate that monetary aim in a 12 months? How loads will you need to make weekly?

How a good deal do you need to make each day? Here's a take a look at how you may discern this out to help you obtain your dreams.

To discern this statistics out, you need to recognize how many days you're going to artwork and plenty of heaps time you're going to take off artwork.

This is critical records, because it impacts your in keeping with day and in line with week price.

Next, think about the current purchaser pricing model that you have in area. Do you have were given periods or profits but? If you don't, you'll need to create a base method that you may paintings from, counting on what you desire to price to your services and products, which can be completed at a later component (this can be addressed later).

Next, we're going to have a look at the NET amount of money which you need to herald after costs are paid. Think approximately the proportion of diverse kinds of periods that you need to do. Do you want to do one hundred% family photos, 100% weddings, or 100% new toddler pix? Maybe you want to do 50% weddings and 50% families, or some different aggregate of different forms of classes. It's critical to understand this data so that you can establish the time and net income restraints for what you need to do.

Now, you want to have a take a look at your yearly internet profits, after which divide that through way of the kind of snap shots classes which you plan to do in the coming year. After you recognize this, you could destroy this down in addition into the kind of weeks that you plan on operating. This will assist you parent out how many education you will need to do for the yr, for each month, and for every week to gather your photos industrial employer goals. It may also help you parent out how an awful lot you need to net for each pix session.

Here's an example:

You're favored internet income is $a hundred,000 for the 12 months

You plan to spend 50 weeks walking

You want to do a most of 200 photography periods

If you're running the ones numbers, in case you're going to make $one hundred,000 in 50 weeks, you may need to make $2,000 each week.

Divide your favored internet income thru the 2 hundred images periods you need to do ($100,000/200), and you'll discern out how thousands you need to make consistent with session. In this situation, you could need to make $500 on each session which you do.

Then, in case you comprehend you'll paintings 50 weeks within the three hundred and sixty 5 days and you intend to do hundred pictures periods within the 365 days, you recognize that you have to do a mean of 4 periods each week, this means that that a median of 16 education each month.

With this approach, you're capable of find precisely what you need to do each week and each month to ensure which you obtain your final reason of making a net income of $100,000.

Discovering Your Cost of Doing Business

Of path, you furthermore might also want to test your modern or planned enterprise enterprise charges so you can parent out your price of doing enterprise. Your agency fees will in shape into categories: steady fees and variable expenses.

Business licensing fees

Consistent, shrunk advertising and marketing and advertising and marketing and advertising and marketing fees

Fixed Business Expenses – Fixed business corporation fees are ongoing business corporation expenses that are not going to trade in the destiny. Some examples of those expenses embody:

Insurances

Internet service

Memberships

Permits

Studio rental

Website internet website hosting

Other annual, monthly, weekly, or every day fees

Variable Business Expenses – Variable commercial enterprise enterprise corporation prices are prices that could range and range over the years. Examples of variable fees also can encompass:

Cost of bundle deal deal gadgets

Cost of printer toner or paper

Equipment renovation

Equipment alternative

Estimated taxes

Gas costs

Hiring an assistant

Office additives

Toiletries

Utilities

Vehicle upkeep

After you provide you with all your consistent and variable prices, you may want to offer you with a entire of your anticipated annual charges. Then you may harm this variety down into the charge of doing commercial company month-to-month, weekly, every day, and consistent with photos consultation.

Pulling it All Together

Now, allow's pull all this financial information collectively. Combine your charge of doing enterprise with the net earnings which you want to make within the subsequent twelve months. This will assist you make a decision the real base fee that you need to make for each photos session which you need to do.

Once you apprehend what you need to make for every images session, you can apprehend which you can not tackle photography classes so as to pay you lots much less than your baseline. If you do, you can in no way be able to acquire the dreams that you have set for your self, and also you'll work tough on the same time as not having any terrific of lifestyles or earnings to show for all your difficult art work.

Creating Your Daily Schedule

To accomplish your dreams, you need to begin developing a every day time table.

Following a each day agenda is a way that many entrepreneurs and small commercial organisation proprietors have used with remarkable success. If you do no longer focus on a each day time desk that permits you take steps towards your goals, you'll find out it difficult to attain each quick and long time desires.

Every day, you want to begin at zero. What does this imply? It technique that each, unmarried day, you need to come back to work and paintings in the direction of the destiny as difficult as you do some different day. It does now not rely how well you trust you studied you're. It does no longer depend how smart you're. It does not rely how busy you are. You commonly should paintings tough – you could't give you the cash for to slack off at any thing. When you have got got this mind-set each day, you'll keep away from most of the peaks and valleys that many small commercial enterprise owners revel in as they're trying to acquire achievement.

What Your "Perfect Day" Should Include

What have to your "nice" day include? Here's a examine what you need to consist of in every day.

Time for Learning – No rely how brilliant you discovered you're at strolling a enterprise or images, you have to constantly hold getting to know.

Learning maintains you on pinnacle of new traits on your vicinity. Learning helps you to discover new strategies that you could use to construct your business enterprise. If you want to increase your commercial enterprise employer, you want to develop, and analyzing is the crucial thing to developing.

Practice Time for Your Sales Presentations – We have already looked at how crucial it's miles to spend time schooling your earnings indicates. Regular workout will assist you growth everlasting competencies, so ensure that you exercising your shows daily so that you enhance your abilities and revel in stepped forward profits.

Businesses Building Tasks– You may also moreover want to take time every day to take care of duties that assist you assemble your organisation, which encompass prospecting and monitoring your outcomes. Some of the important business organization building duties you'll want to engage in every day embody:

Lead Generation – While it is crucial to make use of the leads which you already have, you'll want to spend some time on lead era day by day so that you keep growing your organisation with new customers.

Contacts Goals – Each day, you'll want to spend some time contacting your leads. If you do no longer have touch desires each day, it's going to probably be hard to turn those leads into paying customers that help you gain your photography commercial enterprise goals.

Appointments Made – Part of turning leads into customers consists of making appointments. You need to get leads to enroll in appointments.

Spend time in this daily.

Sessions and Consults Performed – Most days ought to consist of sporting out snap shots lessons and/or photographs consults.

Remember, your instructions and consults are an vital a part of generating profits for your business business enterprise.

Appointments with Signed Clients – Of course, you have got already got signed customers that you may be wanting to make appointments with regularly.

This also can include viewing appointments wherein you allow your clients view the pics you've got taken, providing them together together with your income programs.

In Person Sales – You want to moreover have interaction in in individual income each day, an superb way to assist you to gather a successful pics industrial employer.

Replying to Calls/Emails– Some of it slow each day want to be spend replying to cellular telephone calls and emails. This can also embody doing:

Lead Follow Up – Spend time replying to calls or emails that come from leads. It's additionally important to deliver emails or make calls to leads to conform with up with them, regardless of the truth that they've got no longer asked any questions or requested for help. Following up is commonly vital. The greater you look at up together at the side of your leads, the more likely you are to transform a lead proper right into a paying patron.

Client Follow Up – You may additionally need to spend some time following up with current-day clients. If you've got got already finished the consumer's photography session, you may want to comply with as lots as time desk a viewing appointment. If your purchaser has already ordered merchandise, you can comply with up, letting customers recognize at the same time as to anticipate their order to be introduced.

Past Client Follow Up – Don't forget about to spend time following up collectively together with your beyond customers. Yes, new leads are crucial, however it's easy to get repeat sales from beyond customers who're already very happy along side your art work.

Spend time each day following up with past customers, seeing if they have any new desires with which you can assist them.

Chapter 4: Recording Your Hours Worked

Creating and following a each day schedule is vital, however you moreover might also want to ensure which you record all your hours that you art work. Keep a pass browsing paper or for your laptop of all the hours which you paintings, whether or not or now not you are spending time taking photos a patron's session, processing orders, editing images, or searching out new leads. Your time is essential.

Why need to you file your hours? It's essential in case you want to song the numbers of hours you're going for walks each week, month, and 12 months. You moreover want to keep tune of each different numbers. As you record your hours and extraordinary relevant information, it lets in you to better track your non-public effectiveness and conversions.

Tracking records is always a effective tool as it offers you a better take a look at how your employer is appearing. You'll be able to find areas in which you can make enhancements. Maybe you could locate strategies to automate responsibilities so as to reduce the hours you need to paintings to make the same amount of money. Perhaps you will discover that you're no longer making sufficient conversions, and you need to adjust your every day time table to end up greater powerful. Remember, the extra information you have got were given, the better organized you're to track your improvement and make any crucial modifications, making it easier that allows you to gather those long term goals.

Focusing at the Business Leads You Already Have

Make effective that you spend hundreds of time focusing at the economic employer leads that you already have. Many photographers make the error of being so centered on generating commercial business enterprise that they in fact forget about the leads that they already have and didn't convert within the beyond.

Simply getting to know the way to enhance your income presentation and profits techniques also can moreover assist you beautify your effectiveness, that may propose that you need fewer consequences in get the same big form of paying clients. You need to discover ways to paintings smarter with what you've got were given. It will take a good deal much less time and effort to enhance your strategies to promote to fashionable-day leads than it's going to to discover and try to convert new leads. Do not permit your errors or loss of statistics make it greater difficult on the way to gain your goals and the achievement that you need in your photos industrial enterprise organisation.

Remember the residence analogy? Now is the time to create new robust partitions of dreams, course of action, and a each day time desk to gain achievement with your pics commercial organization. Do not grow to be like many photographers who end up going out of enterprise in a extremely good deal much less than years. By using those techniques, that have verified to be effective for lots unique entrepreneurs and small enterprise enterprise owners, you may also experience the fulfillment which you want. Remember, you need to be inclined to paintings hard and you want to art work tough every, single day. You must set particular, sensible, and attainable dreams. You will want to format a plan to help you take steps within the path of those dreams each day, each week, and each month. Then, you may need to create a each day plan that you can look at every day, ensuring which you entire the obligations that need finished to experience reaching your dreams.

You are on your way towards constructing your a fulfillment and profitable photographs commercial agency. Don't surrender putting in those new walls in an effort to be the power of your pics business organization!

BRANDING AND MARKETING YOU AND YOUR PHOTOGRAPHY BUSINESS

You've were given a latest basis through eliminating vintage commonplace errors. You've built new walls of shape via desires, motion plans, and a every day time desk. Now it is time to attention on how your customers will see you with a easy branding and advertising message. If we live with the house analogy, it's time to start putting in the house windows of our residence, so our clients can see honestly as to how our pics company can help them.

Most photographers in no way don't forget the branding and advertising and marketing and advertising element of beginning a new commercial enterprise, but, every branding and advertising are critical to the fulfillment of your photographs enterprise. Failing to logo and marketplace your business enterprise will probably result in failure of your industrial corporation inside a 12 months or .

With best branding techniques and advertising and advertising expertise, you have got have been given the capacity to expose a startup images organization proper proper right into a booming business enterprise speedy. If you're not remarkable in which to get started out, this bankruptcy will help you observe the basics.

So once more once I out of place the entirety, I became in survival mode and I come to be doing what every other photographer does: going after the entirety and some thing. As an instance, I went and signed up for the nearby newspaper and weekly e-book. I became getting $50 gigs and $35 greenback gigs, only for survival. I apprehend some of people are available and are doing the same aspect counting on what their way of existence situation is proper now...Anybody is distinct. Those gigs genuinely helped me live on at that thing as soon as I wished it.

The detail is despite the fact that, long time you can't live on off of that form of coins. At the prevent of the day even as you pay your bills, you pay for your gas, you pay to your time, and you pay for your living charges, if you are really making $35 or $50 a gig, you are in no way going to get earlier. You in no way are going to have the capacity to shop for the equipment or be able to do any of the property you need to do as a professional photographer. I determined myself in that equal situation. It modified into like irrespective of how tough I labored; I turned into entering into that identical cycle.

So I emerge as going into the holidays after 2008 as soon as I out of place the entirety and feature emerge as reinventing myself and I sat once more and perception, "What's going to break up me from the competition?" Everybody has a digicam these days!

What am I going to do? I knew I had to positioned my questioning cap another time on and pass decrease lower returned to my functionality devices that I knew. I had to reinvent and separate myself from all of us else. Coming into the holidays, I knew, correct, awful, or detached, there are humans to be had that spend cash to get their photo desirous about Santa Claus. In my head, I kicked and screamed! I did no longer need to try this due to the fact I idea I became promoting out, selling my soul. I did not want to be like absolutely everyone else. But the extra I dived into it, the more I concept, I do now not should be like each person else. I want to split myself from every person else with the beneficial aid of coming near this in a few different manner and this is in which I invented the idea of the Santa Experience, it is a completely specific one-of-a-type way that every person has achieved inside the worldwide. This technique helped me from a branding perspective and proper out the gate and it gave me a mechanism to interrupt up myself from anyone else.

You are going to have a have a look at within the rest of this e-book how I leveraged non-earnings and corporate sports and the Santa Experience is likewise one of those gadgets that have been given me into very targeted and unique environments wherein I come to be able to find out and skip right away after a splendid avatar: the humans with the disposable income who could pay for the form of snap shots offerings that I desired to provide. I knew I couldn't stay to tell the tale on $35 a session or $50 a gig. I had to have people in my base that have been inclined to spend hundreds to thousands of dollars while it came to photographs offerings. I needed to separate myself from all people else to be had doing family commands, fall lessons, or maybe very traditional santa periods, so the concept become to split myself from the institution and what helped me circulate in that route turn out to be to create some component in reality unique with the Santa Experience.

Now past this ebook, I can't dive deep into the Santa Experience itself, however I do need to percentage that I honestly have an possibility to observe the route for it. If you visit www.SantaExperenceCourse.Com you may studies more records about that direction. It may be very unique and really specific and it's far greater than only a session; it is a completely interactive enjoy that helped me separate myself from all people else and virtually considered one of many examples that I am going to percent with you on this e book, so flow there now.

DIFFERENT TYPES OF PHOTOGRAPHY MARKET SEGMENTS

One huge mistake many new photographers make is attempting to be all things to anybody. If you try to awareness on each pics area of hobby, you are headed for catastrophe. Think approximately the most a success photographers in the international. What are they diagnosed for? They are normally acknowledged for definitely one or forms of pix. It's very uncommon for a successful photographer to be regarded for servicing all types of pix niches and markets.

Why is it so vital to find your niche or market section? Not exceptional is it plenty much less difficult to excel in a unmarried niche, it's additionally much less complicated to marketplace when you have a selected place of hobby. The smaller your region of hobby, the less difficult it's miles to find out your hole within the market.

Let's begin searching on the unique kinds of photographs market segments, or niches. There are cutting-edge photographs classes: company and client.

Most photographers decide to move one course or a few different. While there may be a few crossover among business and patron snap shots, the most successful photographers are usually recognised for one or the alternative. In many instances, they have got a selected place of interest in a single or two genres.

Looking at the various pictures marketplace segments allow you to apprehend what options are available to you. When you're acquainted collectively together with your options, reflect onconsideration on what you experience doing. What are you suitable at? Will it pay you sufficient? How a exceptional deal competition is there inside the marketplace? Do you want specialized gadget for the location of interest? Does your modern-day area in form the location of hobby you need to paintings in? These are all questions to ask your self when looking to determine on your images marketplace section.

COMMERCIAL PHOTOGRAPHY

Here's a look at a number of the commercial images niches:

1. Photojournalists – Photojournalists spend their time documenting locations, activities, and those who are taken into consideration newsworthy. Their pix may additionally display up in telecasts, webcasts, on-line publications, or print guides. In normally, photojournalists do document to editorial workforce and may carry out a number of unique responsibilities, which incorporates taking pictures film video segments or photos, transferring digital documents to laptop structures, the usage of picture improving software software program, gathering historic beyond records on topics, writing narration to accompany their pix, and

submitting pix and distinct statistics to editorial personnel. Travel to assigned places is frequently required. Unfortunately, even as there are splendid possibilities and specific sports to revel in, the pay is typically low.

As publications keep to vanish, there are fewer possibilities to be had for photojournalists.

2. Headshots – Actors, fashions, and company professionals frequently require headshots for advertising features. Headshots are a selected fashion of portrait that realistically indicates off an individual's look for casting or branding. Headshots can be a portrait of a whole frame or a face with a ancient beyond that enables to expose off the man or woman of the individual that is being photographed. Several forms of headshots encompass:

a . Entertainment Industry Headshots –
These headshots are generally for actors,
singers, and one-of-a-kind varieties of
entertainments. Most of these
entertainers should consist of headshots,
similarly to a resume, once they workout
for jobs. These headshots may be more
artistic than one-of-a-type styles of
headshots and performers regularly have
more than one headshots that function
high-quality expressions and poses.
Performers may additionally have both
theatrical headshots and business
headshots taken.

b . Modeling Headshots – Often known as
tear sheets or comp playing gambling
playing cards, modeling headshots include
compiling more than one photos on one
sheet.

Close u.S. Of americaare regularly required
to expose the version's pores and pores
and pores and skin. Modeling headshots

are regularly used for modeling portfolios, mag commercials, TV advertisements, comp playing cards, on-line business enterprise profiles, and greater.

c . Business/Corporate Headshots – These headshots are frequently used for branding, advertising and marketing and advertising and marketing, and social media. In most instances, topics are handiest display head to torso or head to chest. Corporate headshots can be used for Facebook, LinkedIn profiles, annual reviews, author pages, company internet web sites and courses, resumes, about us pages, newspapers and articles, press releases, and company advertising items.

3. Editorial/Lifestyle – This photography area of interest makes a speciality of telling recollections or conveying mind. This type of pictures is frequently used within magazines. The reason of this images fashion is to tell memories or to

inspire humans with a image. Editorial/way of lifestyles photos regularly combines the preparedness of studio photographs with the candid nature of photojournalism to offer a completely unique, day within the lifestyles look that also has a piece of writing extraordinary.

four. Stock Photography – Stock snap shots has the capability to be a worthwhile place of interest for photographers and this term applies to three of the conventional photographs that you stumble upon from every day. To be successful in inventory snap shots, photographers need to discover ways to shoot with a completely specific twist or from surprising angles. It's moreover critical to think about keywords strategically while taking photos. Photographers need to avoid doing the identical antique photographers that others have performed inside the occasion that they want to obtain this area of interest.

5. Product/Food Photography – Product and food pics is a gap that is nearly constantly in call for irrespective of the united states of the us of the economic system.

Companies commonly want to visually sell their merchandise. The purpose of this type of images is to trap customers to want the object being photographed, so it's critical to well show the product and convey its message. Photographers need to study the topics in immoderate demand, a way to recognition on products with strategic lighting, and to investigate from techniques already being implemented in magazines and different varieties of advertising.

6. Event Photography – Since image is everything for businesses, company

occasion photographs remains an opening that flourishes. This form of pix is ideal for the social butterfly. It's vital so that you can mixture into the statistics, however it's moreover important to have an outgoing persona, due to the fact you'll be round plenty of humans. In oftentimes, success in organization event pics effects in one of a kind possibilities, which incorporates the danger to address government headshots.

7. Fashion Photography – Fashion snap shots is one of the more glamorous snap shots niches, and it often includes taking component with well-known designers, working with style models, and visiting spherical the area. However, it comes with its private set of challenges. Fashion photographers often need to be located near major towns and breaking into the place of hobby regularly calls for being an assistant first. Building proper connections is in reality as essential as expertise in case

you're going to achieve this location of hobby. Being a style photographer calls for full-size technical expertise, along with the use of mild gels, backdrops, strobe lighting, reflectors, and further. Retouching enjoy is also an essential technical component of this images vicinity of interest. Fashion photographers need to additionally excel at self-selling.

8. Architectural Photography – For photographers which have a love and a watch for structure and layout, this location of interest can be an extraordinary combat. Choosing this area of hobby makes it possible to shoot for structure corporations, structure magazines and websites, interior format groups, format magazines, and actual assets corporations. There are multiple sub-niches available as well, which incorporates restaurant photography or real belongings pix.

9. Travel Photography – Travel pictures is a snap shots marketplace segment that involves documenting a selected area's humans, customs, landscapes, data, and cultures. Unlike other pics genres, journey pictures is still underestimated and isn't as monetized as a few special genres. Some of the traumatic conditions that face excursion photographers embody taking photos numerous topics in various conditions, low lighting fixtures, and antagonistic situations. It's frequently very difficult to break into this niche as nicely.

10. Medical Photography – Medical pics is a totally specific shape of pictures that requires photographers to deliver intention, accurate photographs that report illness, injuries, scientific strategies, and operations really. This shape of pics is designed to assist educate, record, and beneficial useful resource in evaluation. Many hospitals and scientific studies

centers have photographers on employees to photo scientific conditions and to preserve searchable databases.

CONSUMER PHOTOGRAPHY

Here's a better have a take a look at the various customer photo niches to undergo in mind:

Weddings/Engagements — Every bride wishes a high-quality bridal ceremony day, and that includes the right photographs to maintain those wedding ceremony day reminiscences. For this motive, wedding ceremony and engagement snap shots is a booming marketplace, irrespective of the truth that there's additionally plenty of competition in this location of interest.

Building relationships is essential on this area of interest. In many times, a exceptional photographer can begin thru manner of taking engagement pics, building a dating those effects in contracts for wedding ceremony pix and anniversary photos in the future. Depending at the photographer and the couple's dreams, a conventional or photojournalistic method to the snap shots may be taken.

Traditional wedding ceremony snap shots typically consists of classically posed photographs. On the alternative hand, a photojournalist style generally focuses more on candid pictures with very little photographer interaction.

Remember, this may be a immoderate stress region of interest that calls for quite some gear, and some photographers even discover that they need to lease an assistant.

Portraits – Portrait photographers usually have their personal studio, notwithstanding the reality that they may pass on location for a few shoots. For photographers that experience one-on-

one interaction with customers, that may be a first rate location of interest to find out.

While some photographers select out to recognition on a couple of styles of photographs, unique photographers may pick out out out to attention on only one form of portrait, which incorporates:

Family Portraits — Some photographers pick out out to attention on family pix, and this sub area of interest is an tremendous desire for photographers who are first-rate with youngsters. Family photographs may also additionally embody in-studio snap shots or on area shoots in natural settings.

Maternity/Newborn — Most new dad and mom need to have pix of their new package deal of satisfaction, and new little one and maternity pictures provide a unique area of interest that can convey in lots of commercial organisation. Photographers can reputation on building relationships with expectant moms with the resource of making specific, lovely maternity pix. Parents regularly want contemporary, lovely pics in their babies, and creative photographers can find out unique methods to show off all of the infant cuteness with excellent effects.

Senior – Senior photographs are vital ceremony of passage for maximum excessive college seniors, and both formal and casual poses are commonly wanted.

This manner that photographers may need to shoot formal poses within the studio and head out for on place shoots for informal poses. Keep in mind, formal senior photos can also moreover need to meet superb necessities to be covered in the senior's yearbook.

Seasonal/Holiday Portraits – Another portrait sub-region of hobby is seasonal or tour pictures. Special Christmas photographs are very well-known, specifically for households that like to position photos on their Christmas playing gambling cards.

Other families similar to to file having the whole circle of relatives together with a holiday portrait that they might treasure.

Glamour/Boudoir – Glamour or boudoir pics is turning into even extra popular, and masses of ladies enjoy feeling beautiful and attractive as they take the ones precise pictures. This form of photographs is designed to have a terrific time the precise splendor of the girl.

Team and Individual Sports – Team and person sports activities sports images has the functionality to be very profitable, specially in areas in which sports activities sports activities are very famous. Team pictures embody all people at the group and are posed by the photographer. Individual sports activities activities photos show of the person players and allow for a chunk more person.

School Portraits – Providing school pix, especially for huge colleges, can supply in masses of enterprise, even though doing college images comes with some demanding situations as well. School photographs are commonly completed in a uniform way and these images are often utilized in yearbooks. However, parents usually have the functionality to order those graphics as well, so taking excellent university pics can convey in extra money in circle of relatives orders. The hassle may be dealing with squirmy youngsters all day prolonged.

Parties/Events – Whether it's a birthday, a Bar Mitzvah, or a retirement party, circle of relatives individuals frequently need to capture all of the crucial moments that encompass a huge occasion or celebration. Outgoing photographers frequently do thoroughly with birthday party and event images. Not notable can photographers capture candid pix sooner or later of the birthday celebration, they can also installation image booths and seize precise photos of visitors collectively. This offers a high-quality way for photographers to sell to more than just the hosts of the party.

Pet Photography – The domestic dog enterprise is a massive employer, such as domestic dog masseuses, domestic dog running shoes, puppy hypnotherapists, or perhaps domestic dog photographers.

Many puppy owners want the very terrific for their hairy pals, which makes pet pix an high-quality location of interest for photographers that simply revel in working with animals. This shape of photographs frequently takes quite a few staying power, as it's regularly difficult to direct and pose animals.

Chapter 5: Identifying Your Ideal Client

Once you have got got described what pix area of interest you're a part of, the subsequent step is to discover your perfect consumer. One of the important cornerstones of your snap shots industrial employer is understanding and figuring out who your best purchaser is. Many new enterprise owners make the mistake of skipping this essential step. They begin a commercial business enterprise and gather a net website online without ever considering their clients, what they want, who they are, the problems they have, or the solutions they want.

Who is an Ideal Client?

An best client is a customer that exhibits a awesome technique to his wishes or troubles in the products or services supplied thru your business employer.

Why want to you understand your exceptional customers?

Shouldn't your enterprise organization be for anyone?

Why want to you restriction your self to as a minimum one kind of client?

Here's an instance. Most companies have ninety% famous customers and 10% ideal customers. However, those 10% of brilliant customers generally make up approximately ninety% of the organization's commonplace profits. That's awesome. If most effective 10% of the complete clients are making up 90% of the entire profits for a enterprise, what would possibly appear of a hundred% of a company's customers were ideal customers?

Let's say your enterprise has one hundred customers, and consistent with the sooner opportunities, first-rate 10 of these customers are perfect customers. Let's say which you make $1,000 a month from every best patron. That technique which you're making $10,000 in keeping with month out of your best customers.

Now, what takes place at the same time as you turn all of your customers into incredible clients? If all one hundred of your customers are terrific clients that spend $1,000 a month, you move from making $10,000 consistent with month to $a hundred,000 consistent with month.

That's a HUGE distinction, this is why it's so important to pick out out and intention your perfect customers.

Create an Ideal Client Profile

Now that you're privy to the significance of figuring out your ideal customers, it's important to understand the way to create an first rate client profile.

Creating perfect customer profiles makes it much less hard so as to land the ones excellent customers for your photos enterprise enterprise organization. The following are a few beneficial pointers to help you to create your very own best patron profile.

Identify Age Categories – Think approximately the average age of your extremely good clients. Are they more younger parents a number of the a while of 25-forty? Are your best clients older retirees with grandkids a number of the some time of 50-sixty 5? When you try to create your fine customer profile, ensure you decide the common age of these clients so you understand the age organization of clients who can be the top notch wholesome to your photos commercial company.

Personal Characteristics – It's additionally essential to think about the non-public characteristics of your ideal customers. By data the person types and private traits of your best customers, you'll be capable of offer you with the language which you need to draw those best clients. Do you want to purpose busy moms, new grandparents, new dad and mom, or big households? For example, likely you'd want to intention busy mothers who don't have the time to take pictures of their youngsters. Those moms can be walking 8-10 hour days and they'll have little down time. The more you realize approximately this first-class purchaser, the less complicated it's far to draw that purchaser.

Wealth Characteristics – You moreover want to consider the wealth trends of your perfect clients. What is the not unusual annual income of your best clients? What is the net in reality really worth of your first-class clients? This is vital; because you want to ensure that your high-quality customers will have enough money the products and offerings that your photography industrial employer gives.

Interests and Hobbies — Think about the interests and pursuits of your great customers. Do your best customers enjoy playing golfing, attending wearing sports, shopping for, and masses of others.? While it may appear trivial to choose out the hobbies and interests of your customers, this information can in fact help your advertising efforts. By identifying the private hobbies of your ideal clients, it's less complex to tailor advertising and marketing and customer events round your first-rate customers.

Family and Professional Relationships — Don't forget about about to maintain in thoughts the family and professional relationships of your incredible clients. This is a crucial, and frequently underappreciated, part of growing a wonderful patron profile. You want to realise what individuals are associated on your ideal clients. Maybe they may be paintings colleagues or circle of relatives members. Finding out greater about the relationships of your clients makes it simpler to make connections together along with your quality clients.

Problems or Needs – It's also vital to consider the problems or desires of your nice clients. What issues do they've and the manner ought to you provide a manner to that problem? Every market has specific want and desires, and also you want to be aware of the want and dreams of your customers so that you can discover tactics to satisfy the ones want and dreams.

Other matters to recollect while growing a remarkable client profile consist of:

Do they use social networks?

How do they choose to pay for items/offerings?

How often do they use the internet?

What corporations do they paintings for?

What do they buy?

What is the everyday family make-up?

What is their education degree?

What is their career?

Where do they live?

Where do they paintings?

Now that we have were given have been given created our ideal patron profile, permit's dive deeper and placed an real face to the client. This technique is called growing your consumer avatar.

CREATING YOUR CLIENT AVATAR

LEARN THE BASICS OF AVATAR CREATION

When you're beginning a pics organisation, one of the first steps you need to take is to create an avatar. Unfortunately, most human beings by no means create an avatar, that would in the long run result in business enterprise failure.

What is an Avatar?

An avatar is the profile of the specific customer you want your pictures business business enterprise to artwork with. It's the idealized example of your enterprise' perfect prospect. After all, you want to marketplace to folks that sincerely need to purchase your services. When people experience like you are speakme right away to them, your marketing and advertising is doing its pastime. The superb manner an excellent way to acquire that is to make certain you marketplace as if you honestly are speaking to truely one character — the client avatar you've created.

Identifying Your Niche Market

Before you start developing your client avatar, make certain you choose out your niche market. Think approximately your pix business enterprise.

Have you selected an opening market?

Do you suggest to focus absolutely on bridal ceremony pics?

Are you making plans to do corporation headshots?

Do you need to surely shoot photos of youngsters and babies?

You need to understand your region of interest.

If you fail to have a gap marketplace, you'll have a difficult time undertaking success.

Defining Your Ideal Client

After your region of hobby marketplace, you're equipped to begin defining the excellent purchaser you need in your images employer. Start with a few generalities. For example, hold in mind your perfect clients. Why do they need your provider? How will they research more about what you're selling?

Creating your patron avatar will flow a piece in addition. You'll be capable of convey to lifestyles your ideal consumer through focusing on the character you're focused on with all of your advertising and advertising and marketing efforts. As you decide to expand your avatar, ensure you're honest, direct, and smooth. It may additionally additionally take some time and attempt to create the client avatar, however it's an critical a part of developing and keeping patron relationships within the future.

Remember, the clients stress your company, so you want that permits you to discover them.

Creating Your Client Avatar – The Basics

As you start to don't forget your avatar, customise the way. You might also additionally want to offer you a call to your avatar. As you begin walking through the machine, it's an amazing concept to attempt to "grow to be" the avatar so that you begin to anticipate and experience as your avatar does. Focus at the info. All the information are essential. You want to apprehend your avatar's strengths, weaknesses, life-style, likes, dislikes, and multiple distinct factors.

It's smooth to make the mistake of surely viewing a client on financial phrases. However, it's the relationships as a manner to assist your commercial employer to be triumphant, so that you need to get to understand your consumer avatar as a real person.

You want to recognize their thoughts and emotions. You want to recognize what makes them satisfied or unhappy.

As you get started out, you don't want to be excellent. Simply begin brain storming and writing down topics as you bear in mind them. You can continuously set up this information later.

Outlining Your Client Avatar

One of the high-quality techniques to observe extra approximately your consumer avatar is to start asking some questions. Here are a few questions you may ask to help you provide you with greater statistics on your best customer.

Do they have got any children? If so, what are their a long term?

How may want to others describe your avatar?

What are the hopes and desires of your avatar?

What are the pinnacle priorities of your avatar?

What career is your avatar involved in and what are his/her obligations on the task?

What is the age of your avatar?

What is your avatar's gender?

What is your avatar's marital recognition?

What types of photos offerings does your avatar want?

What matters does your avatar fear about or worry?

What kind of community does your avatar paintings in?

What will make your avatar's existence higher?

Where does your avatar artwork?

Now that you apprehend the basics and the personal statistics of your avatar, you need to begin thinking about what should make your avatar's lifestyles better.

Take the time to without a doubt don't forget your avatar and what he/she wants to do to interrupt the modern-day life cycle. Be particular about the matters that could make your avatar's lifestyles better. How are you capable of help make your avatar's life higher? You want to discover what you could provide on your avatar that they actually need.

Multiple Avatars May Be Needed

While developing a unmarried avatar for now can be exquisite, through the years you can want to provide you with a couple of avatars whilst you run unique advertising and advertising campaigns. For instance, if you decide to offer a couple of services or products, you can want to have separate avatars for one-of-a-type products or services you provide.

As you create the avatar, make certain you have got fun. You may additionally even need to expose it right into a tale. When you get creative, you'll paintings smarter, maximizing your outcomes.

What is Branding?

What is branding? It's lots extra than handiest a brand. It's the perception that clients have of you and your employer. You and all of your advertising and marketing and advertising and marketing substances ought to constitute and useful aid your brand identification. The key is to emerge as aware about your exceptional client (as stated within the previous financial disaster), and then make certain which you constitute you and your business enterprise in a way as a way to hook up with your amazing clients.

Branding is a mixture of technology and paintings that manages establishments amongst manufacturers and reminiscences inside the mind of your first-rate customers. Branding includes focusing your assets of every tangible and intangible attributes to differentiate your emblem in a compelling, meaningful, and appealing manner in your target market.

Branding should be constant and congruent in every issue of verbal exchange, offerings, merchandise, and advertising substances. This consists of you, as a photographer and organisation proprietor, the way you speak with others, and the way you dress. Remember, even whilst you're off the clock, you're even though representing your logo.

Does Branding Apply to Your Photography Business?

Some new photographers wonder in the occasion that they actually need to focus on branding. Does branding in truth follow for your new pics business enterprise?

Yes!

Branding applies to any commercial agency agency, person, products or services, as long as you have got a transaction that takes region between people.

Branding in reality is predicated on a number of the vital standards of psycho-sociology – the manner that the human reminiscence stores, approach, and recalls records. Failing to create and control your emblem is basically like burying your head and the sand and hoping for the excellent.

Of course, first-rate paintings and relationships are though essential to the achievement of your snap shots enterprise business enterprise. Branding and emblem management can help your pix business employer in lots of techniques, along with:

Building relationships and evoking emotions in capacity customers

Communicating a focused message to help appeal to new high-quality clients

Making your customers loyal on your corporation

The Objectives of a Good Brand

A emblem can consist of a call, sign, layout, term, picture, or mixture of these elements to turn out to be privy to the services and goods of your business organisation, differentiating your agency from competitors. When you begin branding, the intention isn't to get your outstanding customers to pick out you over your competition it's all approximately getting capability customers to appearance that you are the first-rate pictures employer that gives them with a choice to their problem.

What are the objectives of a high-quality logo? A top logo need to:

Confirm the credibility of your organisation

Connect with first-rate customers on an emotional stage

Deliver the message of your commercial enterprise company in reality in a manner that potentialities can without hassle apprehend

Chapter 6: Benefits Of Branding Your Photography Business

randing your pics employer gives a number of blessings, consisting of:

Loyalty and Recognition – Branding your photographs commercial enterprise company offers you the gain of loyalty and popularity. When you brand your industrial agency, people are more likely to don't forget you. A robust brand and emblem/image ensures that clients and ability customers maintain your company image of their thoughts. Even if clients aren't conscious which you offer a positive products or services, inside the event that they agree with your logo, they're much more likely to simply accept as genuine together with your enterprise enterprise, even in relation to unexpected services or products.

Image of Size and Expertise – Quality branding can also deliver your organisation the photograph of duration and records. Many customers associate branding with big agencies which could control to pay for to put money into advertising and advertising and marketing and advertising. Effective branding can come up with an picture of size and information, that is crucial whilst customers are looking for reassurance that your industrial company will in spite of the fact that be in commercial corporation in some years.

Creates a Quality Image – Building a sturdy brand additionally helps you to create a exceptional image on your business organization, for the motive that most consumers see a logo as a part of a business enterprise that suggests off price and extremely good. In most instances, on the identical time as you display people equal merchandise and only one product is branded, they nearly constantly believe that the branded product is of better high-quality. When you efficaciously logo your photographs enterprise organization, over the years, the photo of high-quality to your company will maintain to move up.

Gives Your Business the Image of Experience and Reliability — A robust emblem moreover offers your commercial enterprise the image of enjoy and reliability. Strong manufacturers create the photograph of an established business company that has been round prolonged enough to be widely recognized. If you logo your corporation, your pictures business is much more likely to be seen as a organisation this is professional in photos services and products. You'll furthermore be visible as extra honest and reliable than unbranded businesses.

Easily Link Together Multiple Products and/or Services — By building a strong brand for your pics business, you could without troubles hyperlink collectively a couple of services and products. When you use your brand call on each product or service you offer, clients for one product are much more likely to buy some other product out of your business enterprise.

Chapter 7: Setting Up Your Residence For Business

Since we understand you'll more than probably be strolling your enterprise employer from your property, it's time to have a look at the way to get your location set up and geared up on your business enterprise.

It's one element to have the out of doors of your property geared up for friends to appearance; however it's far a completely exquisite element to have your property equipped for customers. Neighbors have one set of expectations that they positioned upon you, as you live near them, but clients have a very one-of-a-type set of expectations. Customers are searching at the whole lot with a very glowing set of eyes, and they be aware all of the little information that your buddies commonly commonly generally tend to appearance over as they stress past your own home each day of their lives. How is the scale back appeal of your property?

Preparing your private home for customers to return back over is form of like promoting your own home; however, you are absolutely selling your offerings. Customers will phrase the little property you stroll by using the use of every unmarried day. You want to make certain that your property is approachable and welcoming. Make sure the outside is neat in look and looks as if somewhere you will want to visit. How is the landscaping around your house? Is it neat and nicely-saved, or is it developing out of manipulate, whole of weeds without a rhyme or cause to it? Details like landscaping deliver an outward effect of the those who stay inside the domestic, and this could decide what your clients enjoy approximately who they are coming over to fulfill with. Kendra and I actually have constantly mentioned the way it doesn't charge some problem to hold your place smooth. We're no longer saying you want to go out and spend plenty of money to panorama or initiate people, however you want it to be clean and tidy and to symbolize your enterprise nicely. You need to hold the lawn mowed or the snow eliminated in wintry climate, as you in no manner apprehend whilst a consumer goes to return over. Running a commercial organization out of your property may be a burden on you and your own family in case you take it significantly. The burden is maintaining it up and presentable for capability clients to fulfill with you at any time. Even despite the fact that you run your commercial company through appointment handiest, there can be times while clients prevent over abruptly or call and simplest have time to meet proper now, and also you want to drop what you're doing and be ready to assist them.

You additionally need to think about your parking scenario. Is there enough room for likely 3 or four automobiles to park in a place this is without trouble available to the doorway of your private home? You might also have set up an appointment for a pair to come returned over and communicate with you about photographing their wedding, however what you don't apprehend is that each devices in their dad and mom are coming alongside, and they'll be the usage of one by one. It's those sorts of conditions which you need to be organized for and feature time to deal with. You don't want to be available shifting spherical automobiles or distinct gadgets that could prevent them from being capable of park in a available region to go into your home. You need to make it as easy as viable for customers to visit and need to do enterprise with you. In truth, you don't sincerely want it to be smooth; you want it to be inviting and snug for them.

Now that we've prepared the out of doors of the house to welcome our capacity clients, it's time to decide out what sorts of sports will truely be taking area within the home. Obviously, we recognize we are capable of be on foot a agency out of the house, but inner that we need to put together for exactly which sports we are capable of be conducting with our customers. For example, will there be studio art work, are you going to have a viewing/promoting room, will there be a vicinity or outdoor areas in which to perform photograph shoots on the house? You want to keep in mind all of these items as you put together the inner of your home to welcome in your capacity clients.

Let's begin thru searching at studio art work. If you're going to devise on having a photograph studio running out of your own home, there are various property you need to bear in mind. First, you're going to want a big sufficient region to perform photo shoots. This method as a minimum 10 toes. Ceilings and a massive enough backdrop to location an entire own family or probable a huge agency of people in front of. Obviously, you will in all likelihood layout your studio for a robust point like children's photos or headshots and small images, and this is wonderful. But both way, you're going to need to observe the studio area and determine whether it's a few thing you may depart set up all of the time, or if it's a few issue you need to rip down and set up because you want to apply that room for one-of-a-type sports activities in your home or circle of relatives. Will the studio have a separate front for customers to get proper of access to from outside your home? In certainly one of our first homes, we transformed the related -car storage proper into a photograph studio. This labored out nicely as it already had 10 ft. Ceilings, it come to be huge enough to understand numerous backdrops, and we were capable of leave it as a studio and be geared up for customers at any time. Not anybody has a room of their home they will be able to designate as a full-time studio, but the ones are some belongings you want to bear in mind while you do not forget having a studio at your property. While a few humans can also moreover set up a small studio in a basement to start out, one interest you should preserve in mind is that clients may be taking walks thru your private home to get into that basement. This technique you want to continually have your private home clean and presentable just for the client to stroll thru whilst going downstairs for photos. Having your very own studio is a dream of many photographers, and it can be a reality — however you need to put together for it nicely and be geared up for all of the situations you will face in serving your clients with an in-home studio.

Running a pictures enterprise out of your home can even require you to keep in mind the way to gift your art work for sale. Rather it is reserving a purchaser for a selected pix system or showing your artwork for them to reserve reprints, you need to don't forget wherein inside the home you may behavior this form of hobby. Many photographers have what they call a viewing room or selling room. This is a chosen region of the residence as a way to be used to reveal photographs or unique examples of your paintings that you could have framed at the walls while customers come over. Perhaps you'll have example albums out for the clients to check. You also can have many virtual examples available thru a computer or a

TV/display inside the room. This is the location wherein you may meet your customers, so that you need to remember what kind of a room you want it to be. In our previous domestic, we had a room that modified into specific entire-time as a viewing room. We embellished it in a Victorian style, mainly ordered the correct furnishings that we desired inside the room, and created a place that we felt turn out to be inviting, snug and compelling. It became the gap in which our clients felt welcomed in our home, and wherein we must display off our art work in a manner that end up representative of our business enterprise. When you have got a room in your private home specific complete-time for assembly with customers, it's important to set the ambience for on the identical time as you're searching for to make that sale. For your viewing room, you want to do not forget things like track gambling, candles burning or precise fragrances that might be appealing for your customers and create exactly the experience you want them to have. Our entire-time viewing room helped our clients sense like they had been on foot into an actual pictures studio in desire to absolutely coming over to a person's home. We had bi-fold doors to shut off the room from the relaxation of the residence, and this made clients enjoy extra like they were in a corporation putting in region of in our domestic.

The cutting-edge-day domestic we've got doesn't allow for a area dedicated to a viewing or selling room. What we decided to do changed into layout our ingesting location in an inviting way that might allow for easy set-up and teardown of the promoting aids we use even as clients come over. We stay in a domestic placed on an inland lake, so we favored to go along with an "up north" Michigan look and feel. When our customers are available, they input our home without delay into the eating location. We have log fixtures, a knotty pine bookshelf and other "up north" accents that purpose them to feel they may be in a welcoming northern Michigan environment. We usually hold this part of our home neat and tidy so at any given 2d, we are able to pull out our easels and show a few massive, framed pix in conjunction with the albums we maintain on the bookshelf proper inside the dining room. You could have a completely usable room in your house sure to be installation fast for when clients come over to talk approximately business company. Thinking earlier a touch bit will prevent pretty some time and art work ultimately.

Many photographers we comprehend may even use their houses for area out of doors photograph shoots. They each panorama their yards in appealing strategies that purpose them to photograph properly, or they could even use close by parks or public gardens for their photographic landscapes. Having an out of doors taking pics location positioned at or close to your private home may be a splendid gain for on foot exquisite images specials. If you don't experience this is an desire at your current-day domestic, then take the time and get to understand your instant location and environment. We stay in a town that happily has numerous public parks, nature facilities and one of a kind public sights that might effortlessly be used as photographic places. Become familiar alongside side your surroundings and locate places that allows you to art work a good manner to take your clients and provide them that particular photographic experience. It may take a few real investigative paintings to find a unique area that one-of-a-kind photographers are not the use of, but that is a part of the amusing of being an artist and a photographer. Now, again to the house!

Since you'll be the use of your home as a place to behavior your organization, this indicates you'll be inviting the overall public into your private living quarters. Some human beings might be very traumatic approximately letting strangers into their homes. This is a hobby you want to take seriously, in particular because it influences now not best you but your circle of relatives. Is an alarm device needed? At our preceding domestic with the in-domestic studio, we elected to put in a home alarm device. With the inflow of net website online web site visitors in the residence, we felt extra sturdy having an alarm tool present, in particular that made it apparent to our clients that we had an alarm system. We knew an alarm device in and of itself have grow to be now not going to prevent decided burglars; but, it became a very obvious and public deterrent that we displayed and highlighted for every person getting into our domestic. We had stickers on all of the doorways and entrances, and we had movement detectors placed very visibly at the partitions of our studio. Obviously, this is a few component you'll want to hold in thoughts primarily based completely upon the crime charges for your place, the rate of your system and the manner your family feels approximately the residence being used as a corporation.

As this is your house that you are installing location for commercial organization, in all likelihood you don't need customers to move returned over the least bit. This is genuinely an opportunity you can keep in thoughts and also have a a success commercial business enterprise. In in recent times's technological global, there are loads of options for talking with clients however in no manner having to fulfill each other in individual. Years in the past whilst we started our pictures enterprise corporation, I ought to mention that ninety five percentage of our customers — mainly for weddings — met with us earlier than reserving with us. Today that range is appreciably decrease. Kendra estimates that perhaps simplest 35 to 45 percent of our bridal ceremony pics clients in reality meet together together with her. There are a larger amount of clients who are actually reserving over the Internet and now not even speaking with Kendra on the smartphone. It is definitely feasible to run your commercial enterprise enterprise out of your property and by no means have your clients meet you there. There is continuously the selection of zooming or facetime calls with clients to fulfill them and get a enjoy if you are a in form for what they'll be looking for.

If clients do need to talk in individual, there are awesome locations wherein you can meet them, which incorporates ingesting locations and coffeehouses, or maybe civic golf equipment collectively with the American Legion, Eagles, Elks or splendid clubs you will possibly belong to for your network. It's furthermore possible to meet customers of their non-public homes – relying on how snug you are with this concept and what sort of community you live in; this is a few element you may keep in mind. However, regularly you and your customers will experience greater snug definitely meeting at a public place wherein exclusive people are present. We have often met clients at eating places and coffeehouses, especially in the event that they stay out of doors of our immediately vicinity. When you begin your commercial enterprise, you want at the way to take any business business enterprise you may get, due to the reality you need to get revel in and you want testimonials/evaluations from those customers. This way which you is probably strolling out of doors of what is going to in the long run turn out to be your everyday place of tough work. In the start, be prepared and willing to drive anyplace the work can also moreover take you. I virtually have constantly stated, I obtained't lose a marriage photos sale over a tank of gasoline.

If you do determine not to meet customers in your property, you're going to need a earnings package that may be curious approximately you to symbolize your industrial corporation and photographic abilities. The profits package may be created to be very businesslike, or it is able to be very artsy and possibly constitute more of your man or woman. I am a businessman by means of manner of the usage of schooling, so I certainly have generally tended to lean greater closer to what may be considered a very expert look. When I in my view think of setting collectively a earnings bundle, I accept as proper with getting a dark brown or black leather-based-based totally hard-sided bag nearly just like a small suitcase or large briefcase. Then I would possibly fill it with the essentials wished to expose off to my clients that I am a professional photographer and that I am the photographer they need to pick out out out for their marriage ceremony snap shots. If Kendra had been to put together the equal income package, she may additionally choose a few form of bag this is more representative of her innovative person. Kendra is an artist and historian by way of education and has a completely specific concept of the way she may need to want to represent herself with our clients. She uses a crimson leather-based-based bag this is very artsy and has a laugh pens and example art work in it.

When we first started walking together 25 years within the beyond, she used to tell me I even have come to be too technical and uptight with the clients, that I needed to lighten up and feature amusing with them. Kendra changed into certainly proper; I become too technical and severe in representing my pix. My factor proper here is that your earnings package deal needs to signify who you're and what you are taking shipping of as actual at the side of your brand to be.

Within the profits package deal you're going to need to have severa portions of example artwork for the capability clients to view. You need to have your computer/tablet, corporation playing cards, brochures and rate lists. Customers love so you can stroll away with some thing of their hands. The amazing factor approximately in recent times's cutting-edge laptops and capsules is that you can with out trouble put together a stunning slideshow and feature that gambling at the same time as you are discussing your substances and explaining why you are the great photographer to seize your customer's memories. Remember as you're going out to fulfill along with your potential customers to get dressed as it should be for the kind of interest you're looking for. This doesn't imply you need to be in a dress or three-piece in form or a dress, but you need to dress professionally and constitute your self in a way if you want to no longer negatively impact your enterprise organization. You best get one danger for a primary impact – don't ever neglect this!

Another popular choice for meeting clients is to associate with a enterprise corporation that would have similar hobbies within the equal clients you are focused on. For example, if you are normally inquisitive about weddings, you could need to companion with a community florist or dress shop. Many instances, small businesses are greater than willing to hire you a tiny location to satisfy together with your clients and show your paintings. Or if you're searching out greater of a frequently going on region to try this, you could take into account a few thing like a nearby bakery, a community virtual camera preserve, or maybe an art work gallery. Depending on which kind of enterprise you pick out to associate with, the greater options you may have with regards to what form of paintings you may need to show, and which sort of clients you may meet with there. As your business commercial enterprise organisation grows, you could start to shape a community of all brilliant styles of marketers. Don't take those relationships with no consideration, as they may shape a very strong professional community for you in the destiny.

And now at once to the house workplace. This part of your commercial enterprise business agency is so critical that we've got were given dedicated an entire chapter to it.

Chapter 8: Creating The Perfect Home Office

Your home place of work will become the coronary heart of in that you behavior business corporation. You can also be spending numerous time modifying on this location, so make certain to select out somewhere in which you could be content material fabric and efficient.

Working from domestic has come to be such not unusual place now that there are various super gadgets available to make it less complicated for you to finish the responsibilities wished for your property based totally actually business organisation. I encourage you to visit a staples save or an IKEA and truely test the whole lot they ought to equip a domestic place of work. You can be amazed at the creativity positioned into domestic place of business device and the way no longer exceptional stunning it can be however how useful and time saving it is able to be.

One of the maximum important administrative center gear you may use is probably your pc. The computer is used for the entirety from verbal exchange to improving the pix to developing slideshows and YouTube videos which you put together in your clients. Your pc and your digital camera are the 2 maximum crucial gear you'll have as a photographer and a businessperson, followed carefully collectively along with your cell cellphone.

Most humans beginning out have already got some shape of computer and have an idea of what sort of laptop they're cushty the usage of. You don't need to have the most pricey laptop to be had that allows you to run a photos commercial enterprise organisation. It is definitely beneficial which you pick out out one with processing skills that healthy the maximum difficult piece of software program software software program you'll be the use of for your business corporation. More than likely, considering that may be a photographs enterprise you're placing together, the most hard or taxing piece of software program you may use can be your image improving software program software. We use Adobe Photoshop and Adobe Express in our company; however, there are various software program programs available available available on the market in order to artwork for enhancing your pictures. (One distinct enterprise to test out is Canva. Www.Canva.Com) When deciding on your pc, definitely make sure that the processing capabilities are as a minimum as precise as your photograph editing software software application recommends. Since you already personal a laptop, you probable have already decided whether or now not you're a Mac or PC man or woman.

There are many versions between a Mac and PC, now not great inside the way the pc structures carry out however additionally of their actual computing talents. Many business enterprise owners will lean within the course of a PC because of the substantial form of programs/apps which are successfully to be had to use in taking walks a agency on a PC. However, as a photographer, you are not simplest a businessperson but furthermore an artist, so that you might be attracted to taking walks your business enterprise on a Mac. It is your personal choice to your desire of which format laptop you select out. Whichever one it is, honestly make sure it will do the task you want it to do.

In our company, we positioned it less difficult to have one system committed to image improving and one tool committed to all different corporation obligations associated with the pix business employer. As you grow your commercial enterprise company, you could need to apply your computer for numerous wonderful duties, lots of them at the identical time. We find out it's far first-class to have one tool dedicated to a few factor is taking place with our photographs so that we will have some other gadget open for answering emails, on foot at the internet site or doing a multitude of different duties you address whilst jogging your business enterprise. In the beginning you might be capable of do the whole lot with one tool, but a 2d computer is a few element to don't forget in some time while you in fact begin to get busy, and also you need to multitask. However, as our mobile phones get more powerful and function more skills, a number of the customer service features may be achieved right for your phone. Everything from e-mails, to texts, to even sending out invoices from your QuickBooks app. No count number which era you select to include, or how lots of them you've got, there are a few vital pc necessities which might be critical in order to have your a fulfillment pics business enterprise organisation.

Some of these necessities encompass an outside lower lower again-up difficult strain. Backing up your artwork and your company documents is surprisingly crucial. (The cloud is likewise an option right right right here. We love dropbox.) I can't stress enough that that could be a dependancy you need to get used to if you aren't already. When I changed into in college returned inside the overdue Eighties, I became writing a paper at my brother's residence because he end up the best man or woman I knew who truly had a pc. I typed away at my paper for plenty hours and it come to be coming alongside very well at the same time as all of a stunning, the strength went out and the computer near down. My niece Jill, who modified into very younger at that factor, probable perhaps 5 or six years antique, emerge as playing at the family's electric powered powered powered organ and blew a fuse within the basement in which I end up walking. Thus, I determined out my lesson in backing up all of my precious documents. You may also moreover even want to spend money on some thumb drives in one among a type garage sizes, relying on the form of images work you're delivering. USB thumb drives are pretty cheaper and certainly definitely worth the funding as regards to backing up or delivering your treasured documents. As , your pc furthermore might be used as one of the number one techniques of communique on the aspect of your clients. Email is an vital form of conversation through your computer.

I'm high-quality you're familiar with e mail now, however even as you're the use of it for business agency you need to reflect onconsideration on what kind of e-mail software or format you'll use. One of the most popular organisation-based totally definitely codecs is that of Microsoft Outlook. Microsoft Outlook includes not only an email software program application, however moreover an exceptional calendar and project software program inside it. This may be used at wonderful lengths in now not best speakme together along with your customers, however additionally dealing with the diverse responsibilities associated with your company. Microsoft Outlook isn't an cheaper software, but many enterprise corporation owners locate it well worth the fee in case you in reality discover ways to use all of the gadget it gives.

Another famous manner to talk thru electronic mail is to apply Google's Gmail. Google has put together a very thoughts-blowing on line package deal deal that can consist of now not best your email but moreover a effective calendar that can be used to assist put together your industrial corporation and appointments with your customers. Many of you will be acquainted with Gmail already and are currently the use of it. As you recognize, there are a number of email programs and Internet internet web sites to be able to allow you to use e mail and communicate alongside aspect your customers. It is as an lousy lot as you to decide which program is great for you and will preserve your agency prepared and a fulfillment.

Once you settle on an electronic mail format, one of the first things you want to do is to create a preloaded signature as a way to be on all of the emails you ship or reply to. The signature is a very powerful device in that it now not incredible recognizes the prevent of the message, but can also comprise your cope with, telephone range or every one of a kind touch statistics you would like to offer in your clients. You may additionally even use it to promote specific services or organizations you could have. It is also useful to embody a hyperlink for your internet website online or social media internal your signature so your clients can easily access those very effective machine of your agency.

There are several packages you'll want to load onto your pc, however I'm going to spotlight only some greater that we find vital in walking our pics agency. You are going to need to research a application along side Microsoft Office or a comparable product that consists of a phrase processor, a spreadsheet software program application, and moreover a progressive utility similar to Microsoft Publisher. There are many packages available that embody all of these forms of equipment, however whichever one you select out, ensure it's far nicely matched with Microsoft document formats. You want at the manner to open Microsoft Word files, Excel files, or Microsoft-based totally absolutely emails. Other packages are well-known outdoor of the Microsoftc-primarily based applications, which incorporates OpenOffice, Kingsoft Office or possibly the famous line of cloud-based totally completely applications to be had online from Google. As to your innovative utility, you may pick out a few thing from an Adobe-primarily based product, which can be expensive, to possibly a Canon-based absolutely honestly product or some other innovative emblem that may be pretty a chunk much less pricey. Feel loose to use some thing you're comfortable with at this factor and discover ways to develop into the extra complicated and pricey packages as your enterprise and your skills grow. Obviously, due to the fact that that is a pics industrial enterprise, you're going to need a image modifying software program software software program or suite. We currently use Adobe Photoshop & Adobe Express, but there are some virtually splendid much less highly-priced packages to be had, at the side of Canva or Gimp, so as to do most the whole lot you want to cope with easy picture improving. There also are some fun applications to be had, at the aspect of InPixio, a good way to make it very easy to expose snap shots black and white or add frames or particular lights consequences. Start in which you experience comfortable and are inner your budget, and once more, as your business organization grows and your skills grows, so can your repertoire of software program software software.

The subsequent area I would really like to percentage with you is what I name geek pointers. I can be the primary to tell you I am a whole geek. This has are available in very on hand in the photographs international, no longer only from the technical aspect of the digital digicam but moreover from mastering computer structures and pc programs. I'm going to understand some things I assume will provide you with a piece of a competitive issue on the subject of walking your commercial enterprise business enterprise so you may moreover have a leg up at the competition with regards to your computer continuing to run correctly and cleanly. There is an top notch software application referred to as CCleaner made by way of way of a company called Piriform. You can download a free model of the software program at www.Piriform.Com/ccleaner. (A paid version is likewise available and particularly advocated.) The CCleaner software allows eliminate pretty some the quick files and special documents to your pc which are picked up and left in the back of at the same time as you're at the Internet or the usage of diverse packages. It additionally allows to do away with a number of the capability "parasites" which can infect your pc and rob it of processing power. I hold CCleaner on all of my computer structures and have it set to automatically run every time the computer begins up. I furthermore use CCleaner to hold cookies at the pc which are associated with programs or web sites I frequently use or visit. I can also need to signify you to grow to be very acquainted with the CCleaner software, or one discover it not possible to withstand, and use it to its full capability.

As I am sure you realize, having an superb antivirus or safety software software program software software to your pc is a have to nowadays. You don't should spend some of coins to have a excellent shielding application for your machine. I genuinely have many pals who're IT professionals and feature heard from numerous of them that the easiest manner to defend your laptop is to use what's referred to as Microsoft Defender. It is to be had from Microsoft for as little as $3/month, and I anticipate it's far one of the first-class antivirus applications I even have seen in all my years of running with pc structures. If you surely go to Google and kind in Microsoft Defender for Business, you will discover the internet web page in which you can download this for your laptop. You might also want to remove your current-day or present virus scanner previous to putting in Microsoft Defender, so please observe the installation commands earlier than you circulate in advance with placing this utility in your pc. If you have got already got an antivirus software you're satisfied with, experience free to preserve using – I truely provide this as my preferred opportunity and as a geek.

Thumb drives, or USB drives, are first-rate compact drives to have accessible so you can once more up all of your spreadsheets or enterprise-associated files. We have out of place whole difficult drives on our computer systems earlier than, and a number of our organization files were out of region collectively with the hard electricity. You do no longer want to go through this painful revel in. Purchase more than one thumb drives to maintain as portable backup gadgets, and it will spare you some of grief in the long run.

I'm high quality you have had been given heard of the cloud. The cloud is an internet region to which you may upload your files, pix or any form of laptop documents you want to keep. There are many corporations supplying this shape of backup carrier. One that has been spherical for the longest amount of time is Carbonite. Simply visit www.Carbonite.Com to have a have a look at the special applications they provide that will let you add to the cloud and backup your documents to an offsite place. If you've got already got a corporation you determine with for off-net web web page backup or a cloud-type storage system, ensure they will be expert and may be round in the end. The disadvantage of using cloud garage is which you need to have a completely excessive-speed Internet connection. The upside to the usage of the cloud is you can connect to it anywhere that you may hook up with the Internet. This may be a large advantage in case you journey masses or connect to the Internet from severa particular locations. A fantastic cloud-primarily based software program to load on all of your computer systems is Dropbox. This carrier starts offevolved you out with a free amount of storage and allows you to save your valuable documents out at the cloud and get admission to them from any computer loaded with Dropbox. We LOVE Dropbox!

The last piece of geek advice I am going to provide you concerns locating a good computer technician. I need to don't forget a good computer technician as being without a doubt as important as a very good car mechanic. You want an remarkable manner to consider them, rely upon them, and realise they're not ripping you off with unneeded preservation. Again, one of the pleasant strategies to discover a well computer technician is to ask round for your pals and own family.

Find out who they may be the usage of and who they take shipping of as proper with. You want to discover a person who's expert and honest with the entirety that is to your laptop. Keep this in mind whilst searching out a computer technician — make certain you sense cushty with them having access to everything for your pc. I turn out to be lucky for many years in that my brother Tim turned into a chunk of a pc genius, and he had his very very personal computer restore enterprise. I went to him for pretty an awful lot any type of computer problem, and I determined hundreds from him. Unfortunately, my brother exceeded away awhile returned, and we decided ourselves having to investigate and find out a today's computer technician. We ended up going with one of the companies that has been spherical longest in our town, and we're very pleased with the issuer we acquire from that business enterprise. Having a top notch laptop technician will maintain your corporation up and jogging and lessen the blow of laptop issues as they inevitably will rise up. Hopefully those geek pointers will will can help you have smooth sailing close to jogging collectively along with your computer.

Chapter 9: Finding The Right Photography Equipment

When I first started out out in professional photos, I could critique my photographs as I have come to be on the brink of supply them to my customers. I must note small records like shadows subsequent to my topics from wherein I had have become my digicam vertically, and such things as this definitely troubled me. Shadows are a not unusual critique of professional photographers, however we're able to all be our very own worst critics, and thru starting out with the proper digital virtual camera gadget, you'll avoid masses of the commonplace mistakes which might be made on the begin of a images career.

In my enjoy, one of the pleasant strategies of locating which gadget to shop for is to community with specific photographers that you recognize and apprehend. This ebook is an extension of your images network. And in this bankruptcy, you're going to examine what we keep in mind to be the fundamentals of professional snap shots device. Obviously, the form of snap shots you are going to do will decide how a super deal or little of this device you could need to purchase. The machine you want is some issue you may should determine on as your industrial business enterprise starts offevolved offevolved offevolved out and grows.

Every expert images organization starts offevolved out with the virtual camera. The virtual digicam is the primary device for photographers to particular themselves with photographic photos. I commonly used to say it wasn't the virtual virtual digital camera, but it have turn out to be the photographer that created exceptional pix. And there are often once I take someone's digital camera or phone and shoot pictures with it, and people rave about how remarkable the images are. It is real there may be a talents to images, but having the proper digital camera will make your ardour a pride to experience every time you take photos. The virtual SLR virtual camera frame had grow to be the identical antique for expert photographers all over the global. These kinds of cameras are brief being modified with a few aspect known as the mirrorless virtual camera. A mirrorless digicam doesn't appearance proper now thru the actual lens but uses an virtual viewfinder to expose you what you could capture with the digital camera. It additionally has numerous fewer moving components than an SLR virtual camera. You will need to determine which street you need to transport down based totally in your research. For the ones of you that don't recognize the distinction, SLR stands for unmarried lens reflex; it's far a fantastic form of body and uses a single lens which you are simply searching through as you're taking your pictures. Basically, there may be a reflect within the digital digicam that permits your eyepiece to look via the lens and as quickly as you hit your shutter button, that reflect folds up and out of the way for the image to return through the lens and be captured on the CCD. We presently use Nikon cameras in our organization; however, I didn't start out with Nikon cameras. At the time, I didn't have the rate range to have enough cash a pleasing Nikon camera, so I began out my profession taking pictures with a Pentax 35 mm digital virtual digital camera. Obviously, photographers beginning out in recent times are going to be using virtual cameras. There are many unique manufacturers of digital cameras available within the market. My first rule in selecting an excellent virtual camera is that I want the business organisation that artificial it to be acquainted with pix. The digital camera is a protracted manner more than certainly an virtual system used to take snap shots. It is a photographic tool used to create snap shots in a completely technical layout, and the agency developing it needs to understand pics. I would say if you could start out with a Pentax, Olympus, Canon, Nikon or Fuji logo digital digicam, you'll be beginning out with a chunk of system that is aware of the way to take a nicely-lit, well-balanced image. One of my favored web sites to investigate new cameras with is DPReview. (www.Dpreview.Com) This net website does an fantastic challenge of reviewing several cameras, and you may get as technical or non-technical as you need in inspecting the critiques. I in particular just like the remaining page of every in-intensity assessment, which gives specialists and cons of the specific model. What you need to look for in an notable digicam wherein the white stability and ISO controls which can be with out problem accessible. These are very critical pieces of the photographic puzzle at the same time as you're taking pictures an occasion or just a clean photograph shoot. There are many high-quality web sites to buy camera gadget on; however, I pick out B&H Photo and Adorama as the two top web web sites I often look over for modern pictures gadget. It is likewise incredible to test the producers' net web sites, due to the truth this will provide you with an concept of what can be coming out in the near future. I actually have listed inside the all over again of this ebook all sorts of facts and internet web sites that can help you with this.

Now that you have sold expert photographic device, you want a case or a bag to protect it at the same time as you're wearing it spherical. This is wherein private choice really is to be had in! Kendra loves having a bag that looks as if a wonderful, immoderate-end dressmaker bag, whilst I need to have one that looks greater utilitarian and stronger. It doesn't rely which style you pick out as long as you select one so that it will protect your camera and deliver your device efficiently. Have some a laugh with this and enjoy seeking out your new virtual virtual digicam bag. Inside the camera bag there are some topics I should advise you commonly have with you. I always deliver two quarters with me and generally a few form of multi tool. Both are available handy for tightening screws or camera mounts or one of a kind subjects you may run into while you're out inside the difficulty. We'll get into extra subjects that move within the digital camera bag a touch later.

You additionally need reminiscence playing playing cards. There are numerous types and kinds of reminiscence gambling playing cards available if you need to select out from. I urge you to apply super pinnacle emblem memory gambling playing playing cards and preferably professional grade if you may have enough cash them. Many of the expert grade playing playing cards even will consist of a recovery software, genuinely if you by means of danger layout the card or have a malfunction. The reminiscence card is a in reality vital piece of your pix employer in that it captures all of your be simply proper for you and allows you to provide your customers with what they're searching out. The higher the great of the reminiscence card, the higher the threat that if some trouble does skip incorrect, you'll however be able to retrieve your snap shots from that reminiscence card. There are not any guarantees in existence or in pictures, but saving cash on a memory card isn't a sensible preference!

The lens you choose to your digicam will allow you extra creativity at the equal time as taking images your snap shots. The famous lens that consists of a digital camera is often a huge-thoughts-set to midrange zoom. In the antique days of pix, it become said that we would never flow on from one lens till we mastered that lens and positioned the whole lot we have to do with it. Today, lenses are so appreciably to be had or maybe the same old single lens that consists of the digicam is normally very beneficial. My preferred lens is one which is going from massive-perspective all of the manner out to a zoom setting. We currently use 18 mm to three hundred mm zoom lenses on our professional cameras. This seems to be a completely nice variety for taking pix the entirety from huge companies all the manner right all the way down to zooming in on information from afar. You can be inside the again of the wedding ceremony place and zoom in properly around the marriage ceremony couple at a few diploma within the nuptials, or you can be in the front of the wedding birthday party taking images the precept portrait and use the identical lens for each situations. It may be very popular to have many lenses in your cameras nowadays. My expert hassle with changing lenses regularly is that dust can get into your virtual digital digital camera and onto your CCD, that is the piece of the virtual digicam that captures the photo. Many new cameras claim they may be self-cleansing CCDs and market it capabilities that appear to permit photographers to change out their lenses regularly, however I'm a corporation believer that once I location a lens on a digital digicam, it has sealed off the internal of that virtual digicam from getting any contaminants onto the CCD. When you're taking photographs professional photographs, you want to take the best care in ensuring your device is in tip-top form and that you're doing everything you may to provide the brilliant images possible. Switching out lenses, to me, is a hazard and one I will be inclined to keep away from if viable. However, as with the entirety else, that is sincerely as a great deal as you and the way you need to run your commercial enterprise employer. There are also many filters available for digital digital camera lenses. Some of the filters are for pc snap shots, a few are to take away ultraviolet rays from sunlight hours coming within the digicam, and some will make the skies extra blue or do all styles of remarkable things. The most important element I use a camera clean out for is to shield the lens itself from turning into scratched as quickly as I'm cleaning it. Again, this comes lower decrease again to ensuring your equipment is within the fine shape it can be as you're going out and getting cash along with your digicam.

Now you've got were given your virtual digital camera, your lens, your bag and some memory gambling playing playing cards, and you're beginning to appear like a seasoned. Next, we want to look at the outdoor flash in your virtual camera. A lot of photographers in recent times are clearly into generating photos with what they name "natural slight." I agree absolutely that there are situations in which herbal slight gives a positive length to a image that could not be attained every other way. However, an out of doors digital camera flash is your friend, now not your enemy. A real outside digicam flash will help make you numerous coins over the career you have got had been given chosen as a photographer. Now once more, there are numerous businesses available that make a several incredible brands of outside digital camera flashes. A easy rule of thumb we use in our corporation is to apply the emblem we selected for the virtual digital camera itself. Since we shoot with Nikon cameras, we use some of the exceptional Nikon flash devices. They are incredible tuned to the digital digicam body, and they may characteristic certainly with the whole thing that's occurring inner that digicam. Again, this is a easy rule of thumb that we use; there are numerous businesses to be had that make top notch flash products, and in case you're inclined to make an effort to investigate the intricacies of these digital gadgets and in form them perfectly in your digicam body, I am sure you could have extremely good results. Another region that's becoming famous in the outside flash global is having a far flung flash controller that hooks onto your virtual virtual digital camera to then manipulate more than one a ways flung flashes you've got were given set up as your lights. This may be a miles plenty less highly-priced way of getting into expert portrait lighting than purchasing a fixed of studio lighting. Depending on what sort of pix you may deliver interest to, this can be some thing which you want to investigate. We will bypass over actual studio lighting later in this financial disaster, however a ways flung flash gadgets can be quite a effective tool whilst you're out at an event doing portrait pictures, specially in case you ever get into innovative lighting with gels and specific attachments.

At the start of this bankruptcy, I cited one of the pictures mistakes I made changed into having the shadow off to the thing of my trouble as soon as I may want to flip the virtual virtual digicam vertically. One way to effects do away with the shadow is to use an off-digital digital camera flash bracket connected on your virtual digital camera frame. The brand that we like to apply is called Stroboframe. The Stroboframe has been spherical for quite a while and has a totally dependable bracket. Basically, it turns your flash into what I ought to call a flip flash. When you move from shooting horizontally to vertically, your flash stays over pinnacle of your lens and proper now for your problem, casting off those demanding shadows that come off to the difficulty on the same time as you normally shoot vertically. It without a doubt amazes me how many photographers do no longer use any kind of flash bracket while doing portrait work. I can apprehend if you're capturing natural light pictures, but the fine component about the use of a flash all through your portrait pix as it offers the challenge a twinkle of their eye. That twinkle of their eye is one of the trademarks of a professional portrait. Don't be scared of your flash, because it virtually is your friend and might make your pictures step as a good deal because the expert level. The flash bracket for us is an crucial part of pictures system.

Another piece of device that has an inclination to lend itself to the extra professional photographer is that of the tripod. A correct digital camera tripod is to be had in very available while you're doing a whole lot of portrait art work. There are a few schools of idea that say you can't shoot an extremely good portrait without a tripod, however I will go away that as a bargain as you to decide. The better the tripod, glaringly the more money it's going to rate. The brand that we decided on to use in our business corporation is Manfrotto or occasionally referred to as Bogen.

Chapter 10: How To Get Customers Marketing

When maximum humans reflect onconsideration on advertising, they may be taking into consideration advertising. They believe commercials on TV, or the radio, YouTube, or Facebook and that they assume this is advertising. In truth, that is pleasant one portion of advertising and marketing. You may also have the fine photos industrial enterprise organisation within the global, however if you could't train people approximately your business agency and attraction to customers, you will not acquire achievement. For this reason, I am going to offer you with a quick lesson inside the fundamentals of advertising before we get into the specifics of exactly the manner to sell your pics industrial business enterprise.

Marketing one hundred and one: The 4 P's of Marketing – Product, Place, Price and

Promotion. To honestly apprehend a way to market your organisation nicely, you have to apprehend those 4 thoughts. Understanding each one will permit you to help your customers higher understand your business enterprise and also will assist your non-public business and who your clients without a doubt are. Let's start with the product.

Product is what you'll promote. That's what your clients want to shop for from you, and it's how you'll make coins with this enterprise organisation. On the floor, the made from a pix business enterprise appears to be quite easy; they are images. However, in nowadays's pretty competitive pix marketplace, the product extends beyond the actual image itself and encompasses the enjoy your patron has with you the photographer. This is particularly real at the same time as you are photographing an event collectively with a marriage or huge birthday celebration of some type. Your consumer manifestly wants to get keep of first rate pix on the give up of the task, but in addition they need to have a wonderful experience with the photographer as they're going via the way of creating those pics. That's why the product is thousands greater than really the photo or the bodily object you're handing over to your patron. Look deeply into what your actual product is and apprehend it with the intention to certainly understand what your patron is calling forward to from you and what you're definitely offering for them.

Price. Obviously, the rate is what you may be charging for the product and company you're turning in in your purchaser. What is in truth concerned on this price? You have to ensure the rate now not best covers your prices however gives you with a superb enough profits to benefit achievement. When I actually have turn out to be incomes my bachelor's diploma from Northwood University decrease back in the early '90s, I had an teacher from Sweden education my senior level advertising and marketing magnificence. He loved to outline fee as an invite to negotiate. He ought to inform us that placing a fee on a product is not anything extra than a place to start negotiating in purchasing that product. This is in reality a high-quality definition of a fee. When you place your fee for your product, be organized for negotiation at the side of your customers. Don't be insulted via this, because of the fact that is precisely what a price is – a place to begin for dialogue. The price is also set by using the use of way of what you experience is a trustworthy and sincere incomes on the product you are supplying your customer. Our accountant has a announcing approximately this; he says the cheapest region at the block is constantly the primary one to exit of corporation. Now this can now not normally be proper, however in masses of instances, that is the case. Make superb to investigate your opposition and find out what a fair market cost is for the goods and services you are imparting. The pictures marketplace is what we inside the employer world name very "elastic" within the reality that, to a positive degree, in which you placed your pricing will dictate a fine amount of the demand that you're going to get to your product. Thus, the lower the expenses the greater art work you will get, and the better the expenses the a lot less artwork you can get. This is wherein you want to set your price cautiously, because of the reality you don't need to promote your self brief; but, you don't want to price yourself so immoderate that you received't get any commercial agency. You can't examine your images business employer to on foot a normal nine-to-5 hobby in which you're making $12 or $sixteen an hour. That is not this organisation. You are in a organisation wherein humans are paying in your craft, your abilities and all of the investment you've made for your gadget. Be very careful on the same time as setting your fee to make sure which you are getting all the price that you deserve.

Place is wherein you'll offer your merchandise to be had available on the market in your customers. This may seem like a reasonably clean idea on the begin; however, in which you sell your product is a completely pertinent step within the way you market your product. If you had a brick-and-mortar studio, obviously you'll be promoting your product out to the overall public in greater of a retail-type surroundings. Since you're on foot your organisation out of your private home, you ought to test particular avenues to market which might be at your disposal. Obviously, multiple the excellent locations you will visit sell your product is the Internet and social media. We is probably getting deeper into your internet website online & social media later in this financial ruin, however the ones are a couple of the places wherein your product may be offered. The form of snap shots you will cognizance on will direct what form of places you're going to promote in. If you are doing panorama snap shots, for instance, you is probably looking at art work galleries or nice web web sites on line on the manner that will help you to show and promote your paintings. Sometimes you can even artwork with a third celebration along side a distributor a great manner to carry your merchandise and help get them out within the marketplace. You need to evaluate in which you are going to promote your product after which plan your advertising method as it should be to have interaction that precise location for income.

Promotion. Promotion is what maximum human beings remember once they think about advertising and advertising or advertising and advertising. This is in that you map out your complete approach of precisely how and in which you're going to sell your industrial agency. To me, that is one of the greater amusing regions of marketing that encompasses the entirety from your literature for your classified ads and trade indicates, all the way proper right down to having a jacket on the facet of your agency name on it that you may located on and displayed anywhere you pass.